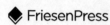 FriesenPress

One Printers Way
Altona, MB R0G 0B0
Canada

www.friesenpress.com

Edited by Sandra Moffat

Front cover: Portal of *Palazzo Gagliardi*
Back Cover: *Papà* on *Via Angelo Santilli* at *Porta San Catalgo*

ISBN
978-1-03-913747-9 (Hardcover)
978-1-03-913746-2 (Paperback)
978-1-03-913748-6 (eBook)

1. BIOGRAPHY & AUTOBIOGRAPHY, PERSONAL MEMOIRS

Distributed to the trade by The Ingram Book Company

MEA CULPA
A Plea of Innocence

a memoir

BRUNO COCOROCCHIO

To *Mamma e Papà*
… may they be resting, peacefully.

N4MARC

Disclaimer:

Truth lies in the senses—*seeing, smelling, hearing, tasting and touching*—of the beholder. As beauty is a matter of personal opinion, so is truth. It, too, cannot be judged objectively, for what one person finds truthful may not be the same for someone else.

This book is a memoir. My memoir. It is my attempt to disentangle the emotions and behaviors that have caused me harm. It is a record of childhood experiences that created triggers in my adult life. The names and places are real, but they emanate from a re-imagined past.

TABLE OF CONTENTS

FOREWORD
by Sandra Moffat, Ph.D.   *xi*

INTRODUCTION
by Bruno Cocorocchio, Age Twelve   *xiii*

CHAPTER 1
L'Addolorata
Mother of Sorrows   1

CHAPTER 2
Nato Morto
Stillbirth   7

CHAPTER 3
Dal Balcone
From the Balcony   15

CHAPTER 4
Rigatoni al Sugo di Carne
Pasta with Meat Sauce   21

CHAPTER 5
La Bottiglia Scivolosa
The Slippery Bottle   27

CHAPTER 6
Pasta e Baccalà
Pasta with Salted Cod   35

CHAPTER 7
Zio Ettore
Uncle Hector   41

CHAPTER 8
Maleducato
Bad Education   47

CHAPTER 9
L'Apprendista
The Apprentice   57

CHAPTER 10
Don Bruno
Father Bruno   67

CHAPTER 11
La Partenza
The Departure   79

CHAPTER 12
La Vulcania
The MS Vulcania   87

CHAPTER 13
L'Arrivo
The Arrival   93

CHAPTER 14
La Prima Abitazione
The First Abode   101

CHAPTER 15
Il Secondo Primo Giorno di Scuola
The Second First Day of School   107

CHAPTER 16
L'Asino di Lavoro
Beast of Burden   115

CHAPTER 17
Tornare Indietro
Going Back   125

CHAPTER 18
Ribellarsi Senza Voce
Rebel without a Voice   131

CHAPTER 19
La Fuga
The Getaway   155

CHAPTER 20
Piccolo Uomo Grande
Little Big Man   165

CHAPTER 21
Fiducia
Trust   173

CHAPTER 22
Figlio di Mamma
Mama's Boy   183

POSTSCRIPT
A Psychotherapeutic Perspective
By Peter DeRoche, MD, Psychiatrist   195

REFERENCES   199

ACKNOWLEDGMENTS   201

MORE ABOUT THE AUTHOR   205

FOREWORD
by Sandra Moffat, Ph.D.

IT TAKES GREAT COURAGE TO WRITE A MEMOIR, ESPECIALLY ONE that deals with a harsh childhood. Bruno takes on this challenge in the writing of *Mea Culpa: A Plea of Innocence*. With tenacity, he describes how growing up in post-war Italy has stifled his self-respect and sense of freedom. At the cost of emotional development, Bruno learns to persevere by emulating his parents' determination and acquires resilience by imagining himself as a Roman centurion.

Bruno and I met in 2005. It did not take long for me to recognize the stoical fortitude with which he confronts life. We married a couple of years later. Soon, however, the destructive forces of Bruno's upbringing began to reverberate in our relationship. He was reluctant to say, "I'm sorry." Arguments were left largely unresolved. Acknowledging this problematic pattern, Bruno embarked on a journey of self-discovery that has provided the foundation of this memoir. Through his writing, I have witnessed the gradual quietening of Bruno's spiteful voices from his childhood and the softening of his guard.

Identities formed in childhood are powerful. Bruno writes that he is haunted by his mother, and sometimes I see her venom in him. I detach, waiting for the loving Bruno to return. In contrast, Bruno describes how his parents, who were embedded in exploitation and sorrow, exuded an endless stream of pain. He had no choice but to absorb it.

I was reluctant to write this foreword because I was afraid of being caught up in the quagmire of Bruno's suffering. While editing his work, I often found myself angry at the perpetrators of his pain. His unabashed writing inspired me to examine my prejudices. And to appreciate his integrity even more.

What I mean by this is that I have learned to value the complexity of the connection between those who have caused damage and those who have suffered from it. Bruno addresses this matrix with a profound understanding of childhood mistreatment. His exploration is crucial, otherwise we run the risk of misjudging the circumstances of trauma.

How then do we tell our stories? Bruno demonstrates that memoir writing helps to deconstruct grief. We can investigate how parental flaws set us up for behavior that does not serve us well. It is the dissection and observation of this phenomenon that makes the writing worthwhile. With surgical precision, Bruno's distinct voice identifies the damage caused by the villains' actions, as well as examines the predicament they are in. It is this sophisticated reflection, from the main character's perspective, that gives *Mea Culpa: A Plea of Innocence* important literary credence.

by *Bruno Cocorocchio, Age Twelve*

Theme

I present to you a person I am particularly fond of: *mother.*

Essay

I want to present to you a person that I am very fond of. This person is my mother. Her name is Elena, she is tall and the color of her eyes and hair is chestnut. I am very fond of her because she sacrifices much for me, for example, she works in a factory that manufactures cardboard. My mother is a simple woman. She is very concerned with my mannerism. When she witnesses rude behavior, she admonishes me with warnings and at times with beatings. Every day when I come home from school, she asks me how my day was and if I tell her that I received a bad mark, she does not let me go out to play and she continuously tells me to study. Because she is a little nervous, she angers easily. Sometime when she's not feeling well, and she notices that the house is untidy, without anyone seeing her, she hurries about to complete the housework. She is not ambitious, in fact she prefers to stay home from morning until night rather than go out to have fun. This then, is a brief presentation of the person I am particularly fond of.

GRADE received: C-

By: *Bruno Cocorocchio*
School Year: *1963–64, Second Trimester*
Level: *Grade 7, Section A*

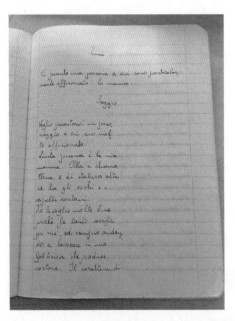

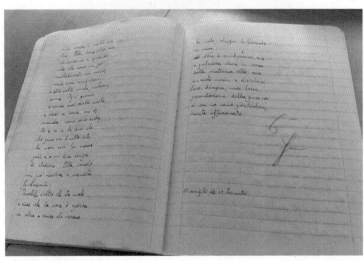

CHAPTER 1
L'Addolorata
Mother of Sorrows

FOR AS LONG AS WE LIVE, *MAMMA* AND I ARE FELLOW INMATES, condemned to a life of misery. Her sentence is based on her stories of misfortune. Mine is based on the false notion that I can make her happy. Growing up in a war-torn country, *Mamma* experienced poverty and famine from a very young age. I was born into a young family struggling to make ends meet, and was immersed in an abundance of shame and responsibility. She learned to fend for herself in a hostile world. I accepted mediocrity in a contained setting.

I see *Mamma* in my eyes. I am possessed. I feel her in my body. She is the millstone around my neck.

Mamma is *L'Addolorata*, my Mother of Sorrows. Her suffering is bottomless. Her pain is unyielding. *Mamma* is *La Regina dei Martiri*, my Queen of Martyrs. Her sacrifices are my accomplishments. Her suffering is my comfort. I am nothing but a porous shield for her torture. In vain, I protect her to settle my debt. Instead, I accrue more guilt.

❀

Mamma is eighty-eight years old. She lives in a care home in the town where she was born. *Mamma e Papà* immigrated to Canada when they were both in their mid-thirties. In their seventies, they decided to return to Italy. They have consistently refused to discuss the inevitable: old age, sickness, and death. Two years ago, *Mamma* suffered a stroke that left her partially paralyzed. She remains confined to a wheelchair and is unable to talk. Six months ago, *Papà* passed away. Although *Mamma* can't speak, she hasn't relinquished her hold on me. Every day I'm drawn deeper and deeper into her quagmire.

I am seven years old, an altar boy. I kneel at the shrine of *L'Addolorata* in *La Chiesa Madre*. The image on the wall depicts purgatory. It consists of three sectors: a fiery hell, a guarded intermediary stage, and a blissful heaven. The middle third illustrates suffering souls in flames awaiting purification before they ascend to heaven. In heaven sits the Virgin Mary holding her child on her lap, her gaze pointed downwards. Her expression is not only of concern but also of compassion and sadness. I identify with the pain of the sufferers as well as the pain Mary feels for those below. In her, I see *Mamma*.

I am twenty-four, a graduate engineer-in-training. It is the eve of my first wedding. I ask *Mamma* if she likes the woman I'm about to marry. She lies when she says that as long as I'm happy, she's happy. It will be our first Christmas as a married couple. My wife and I try our best to see both families over the holidays, but *Mamma* makes it difficult. She is not pleased with our efforts, and her loneliness is too vast to be appeased. Jealous of my bliss, she compares my love for my wife to my love for her, and the time and effort I devote to building my new home to the attention I afford her. She is not happy; therefore, I cannot be happy!

Thursday evening, a week before Christmas, I come home after work to a dark and empty apartment. A note on the kitchen table reads:

"Bruno, I am leaving you. You are not the man I married. Please do not come after me. Goodbye."

Christmas Day. *Mamma* has me back at her table. She comforts me with *"Figlio mio*, today's women are different. Not like us. They are selfish. They don't know the first thing about sacrifice. Not to mention work. They want everything and give you nothing!"

"Non sono più i tempi di una volta.

Quando la donna bilanciava un cestino in testa con un bimbo dentro, ad una mano, una figliuolina attaccata, e all'altra una vanga.

Eh si, la sera se la doveva sciacquare un po' per togliere la puzza del sudore!

Oggi invece, le donne non fanno niente, e si lavano due, tre volte al giorno ... e poi la sera, sono stanche poverine!"

Santa Maria Maggiore— sentito dire da un vecchietto— 13 Aprile 2004

"These are not the times they used to be.

When a woman balanced a basket on her head with a baby inside, and a little daughter attached to one hand and a spade to the other.

Oh yes, in the evening she had to rinse *it* a little to remove the stench of sweat!

Today, however, women do nothing, and wash themselves two, three times a day ... and in the evening they are tired, poor little darlings!"

As overheard from an old man in Santa Maria Maggiore, Sant'Elia Fiumerapido, April 13, 2004

I am forty years old, an accomplished professional and family man. I hold my daughter in my arms as she draws her last breath. Two years have passed since she was diagnosed with a brain tumor shortly after her second birthday. I hand her body over to the undertaker. Sitting alone, *Mamma* sobs. I go to comfort her, for she will not come to comfort me. Her sacrifices far outweigh my pain.

Mamma remains alone. Her husband is dead, and her children live thousands of miles away. She lives in a community unfamiliar to her and shares a room with a stranger. She depends on callous nurses for personal care. Routinely, they change her diaper and move her from the bed to the wheelchair, and from the wheelchair back to the bed. Their instructions are to alert me in case of emergency.

Now and then, *Wilma*, a friend from my childhood, calls on *Mamma* and reports on her general wellbeing. Sometimes she arranges a video call. Today, when she dropped in, the first thing *Mamma* did was to pull at her purse to indicate she wanted to call Canada. Although I'm grateful for the visual contact with *Mamma*, these links always leave me distraught. The screen on my phone fills with *Mamma*'s contorted face. In her gaze, her eyes red and swollen, I see a desperate plea for deliverance, a prayer I cannot answer.

"*Mamma, perchè piangi? Non sei contenta di vedermi?*" My throat constricts as I ask her why she isn't happy to see me. To allay my anxiety, *Wilma* explains that *Mamma* was okay when she first arrived but has become agitated in the course of the call. With those words I feel the sting. *Mamma*, the perennial martyr, has lured me once again into her cauldron. I am torn. I vacillate between forgiveness and condemnation. Awkwardly, the call ends. Neither I nor *Mamma* is satisfied. We wait for *Wilma*'s next visit.

From the moment she gave me breath to the moment she stops breathing, I will be *Mamma*'s willing slave, imprisoned in her darkness. In order to break this collusion, one of us must die. At almost seventy, I remain hostage to her despair. She will not let go. Under a veil of tears, I sense a smirk that says, "You first, Bruno. I am not ready yet."

2016 – *Mamma*

CHAPTER 2
Nato Morto
Stillbirth

I MUST HAVE BEEN IN MY FORTIES WHEN I FIRST BECAME AWARE
of the yearning that had been festering inside me my whole life.
A pining for some lost opportunity—to have been stillborn, and
for my mother to have died while giving birth to me. Perhaps the
moment of recognition was at the breakdown of my marriage, or
perhaps when I lost my four-year-old daughter to cancer. Most
likely, it was a combination of sorts. The culmination of four
decades of failing to rescue my mother from her perpetual afflic-
tion. Had we both died that dreary December morning in 1951,
she would have stopped suffering, and I would have avoided the
burden of guilt that lay in store.

It's a cold and dark afternoon. *Mamma* is eight months pregnant.
For over a week, she's been bedbound. She retains water, and her
legs are swollen. She can't walk or stand. The doctor says she
needs to be in a drier environment. But where? How? The only
place *Mamma e Papà* can afford is this converted pigsty. A bare
lightbulb struggles to brighten the space. Natural light sneaks

through the closed front door. The small window opposite is kept permanently shuttered to keep moisture out. The air tastes like moss. Mold patches decorate the ceiling, and sweat beads cover the walls. It's been an unusually rainy fall. Water rushes in the creek just outside.

Mamma is burning up. She shivers under layers of damp blankets. The mid-wife attempts to comfort her, but to no avail. The doctor drops in and tells *Papà* to take *Mamma* to the hospital because there's nothing he can do for her here. *Papà* goes into town and checks on *Pasquale* to arrange a drive. He stops at *Zio Mario*'s to alert him that we are ready to go. Being older than *Papà*, *Zio Mario* has more experience in dealing with doctors and hospitals. We're going to *L'Ospedale Civile di Pontecorvo*, the nearest public hospital to *Sant'Elia Fiumerapido*, the town where we live. Normally it's a thirty-minute drive, but with the rain it will take us a little longer. *Zio Mario* boasts when he says that, if it was him, he would take his wife to *Roma* instead: "It's less than two hours away, there are plenty of clinics to choose from, and, more importantly, more knowledgeable doctors!" Unlike his older brother, *Papà* has no money, and so he has no choice.

Zio Mario sits in the front, beside *Pasquale*. *Mamma e Papà* and I are in the back seat. It's quiet except for the continuous hum of the motor and *Mamma*'s moans. At the hospital, the doctor confirms *Mamma*'s delicate condition. He tells *Papà* that it's unlikely that both mother and child will survive the intervention. *Papà* is restless. He sits, then stands. He walks back and forth and sits down again. *Zio Mario* and *Pasquale* share pages from a weeks-old newspaper. *Pasquale* reads aloud one of the headlines: "*Una tempesta nel sud Italia uccide oltre 100.*" There was a storm in southern Italy and more than one hundred people lost their lives. Annoyed, *Zio Mario* tells *Papà* to sit down and stop fidgeting. Finally, the doctor reappears. He announces to *Papà* that he has a son and that his wife and baby are both okay but dangerously weak. *Mamma* and I will be under observation and will stay in the hospital for a few days.

Papà recounts the events of the night I was born to his friends, usually over a game of *Scopa*. To set the stage, he gives himself a more decisive role by at first minimizing and then excluding the involvement of his older brother. To add suspense, he pauses in the middle of his story to scrutinize his hand. Assured of every one's attention, he paraphrases what the hospital doctor said: "*Cocoroh*, what's your choice, wife or baby?" Then another pause, with all eyes fixed on him. *Papà* picks a card and as he slams it down on the table says, "*Scopa!* What fucking choice is that? I ask you."

Mamma and I are back in the cave by the creek. *Mamma* continues to feel unwell, and I'm still very small. The doctor tells *Papà* that *Mamma* needs lots of rest and that she should not be living in the pigpen. She also can't breastfeed me because she has no milk. *Papà* doesn't know what to do, so he goes to *Zio Mario* for advice.

Zio Mario is one of *Papà*'s five older brothers. During World War II, he was old enough to be drafted. He was sent to fight on the Russian front and soon after he arrived was caught. As a result, he spent the rest of the war in a concentration camp in Siberia. While there he caught a disease that affected his ability to move, especially his hands. After he came back to *Sant'Elia*, he opened a tailor shop and got married. At around the same time, twenty-one-year-old *Papà* had just completed military service and was looking for work because he too wanted to get married and start a family. It didn't take long for *Zio Mario* to realize that he needed help running his shop. Knowing that *Papà* was searching for a job, he sweet-talked his younger brother into joining him.

For advice, *Papà* always goes to *Zio Mario*, who is now also his employer. When *Mamma* needs to be rushed to the hospital, *Papà* asks *Zio Mario* to accompany him there. When *Papà* has to find a dry place to live, he asks *Zio Mario* to help him and is able to rent an apartment with a fireplace next door to his brother's place. And when *Papà* doesn't know anyone with milk to spare, *Zio Mario* introduces him to a woman who has just given birth to a baby boy named *Pinuccio*.

A year has passed. I have grown. *Mamma* is better, and *Papà* works. But everything is not okay. *Mamma e Papà* argue all the time. There's not enough money. *Papà* blames *Mamma* for spending too much, and *Mamma* blames *Papà* for earning too little. *Papà* works many hours, but the money he brings home isn't enough to pay rent and buy food. *Mamma* has to contribute, so she finds a job at the paper factory not far from town. She leaves early in the morning and comes home late in the afternoon. Because no one else sends his wife to work, people start to gossip. Where does *Mamma* work? Why? What does she do? Does *Papà* know? *Papà's* brothers admonish him:

"*Rucchi*, you got to learn to keep your wife in check or she'll run wild!" When the factory shuts down, *Mamma* stops going to work. And the arguments start all over again.

Papà asks his brother for a raise, but *Zio Mario* says that the shop is going through a rough time and that *Papà* has to wait. *Papà* waits, but *Mamma* cannot, so they argue. *Mamma* says that *Zio*

Mario is keeping us hostage and that he has a hidden agenda—one that does not include *Papà* but his son, *Roberto*, instead. She says that *Roberto* will one day run the shop, not *Papà*. She claims that *Papà* is training *Roberto* to do exactly that—to take over from him. That's why his brother is keeping *Papà* on a very short leash—close enough to make him stay, but not so long to allow him to leave. *Papà* doesn't agree, and every time they argue he storms out the door cursing. *Mamma* sits by the fireplace and cries. I am three years old and feel like I have to do something. I want to help. Most of all, I want *Mamma* to stop crying.

It's all my fault. It's because of me that *Mamma* is always sad and *Papà* is always angry. It's my fault that they're poor. If I had been born dead, *Papà e Mamma* wouldn't argue all the time. *Papà* wouldn't have to be a slave to his brother, and *Mamma* wouldn't have to go to work. If I had been stillborn, *Pinuccio* would be alive today, because I wouldn't have fed from his mother's breast!

Mamma is right, of course. If *Papà* is to be remembered, it would be as, *Rucchitt gliu sart*, Rocky the tailor, the younger brother of *Mario Cocorocchio*, the true owner of the tailor shop on *Via Angelo Santilli*. *Rucchitt* is the one who left for *Lamerica*.

A local proverb: "*Chi n'gózia campa e chi fatìa crèpa.*"
He who negotiates—for example, a storeowner—lives
adequately, whereas he who works—for example, a
day laborer—expires/vanishes.

1955 – *Mamma – Fulvia – Papa – Bruno*

1956 – *Mamma – Fulvia – Bruno*

1954 – *Bruno*, age 2

1957 – *Fulvia – Bruno*

1960s – *La Sartoria Cocorocchio* (The Cocorocchio Tailor Shop)
From left to right:
Zia Maria (wife of *Zio Alessandro*) – cousins *Serge e Daniel* (their sons) –
Zio Vincenzo (Mamma's brother) – *Zio Mario*

CHAPTER 3

Dal Balcone
From the Balcony

PALAZZO GAGLIARDI DOMINATES THE *PIAZZETTA* IN THE OLD HIS-toric section of *Sant'Elia Fiumerapido*. The structure faces *La Chiesa Madre*, the place where the townsfolk congregate to pray. Its large stone portal opens onto *Via Angelo Santilli*, a narrow walkway comprised of massive cobblestones laid down by Roman slaves centuries ago. The edges of the path are perma-nently entrenched with grooves from the thousands of wheels that have rolled on it. When it rains, the wet surfaces make walking treacherous. To the right, the road leads to the center of town and then out onto a network of autoroutes. To the left, it leads down the valley to fertile farmland.

Adjacent to the *palazzo* is a courtyard. In the morning, before the town awakes, farmers line up to sell fresh produce. In the afternoon, after siesta, children gather to toss a soccer ball around or to brandish a wooden stick as a make-believe sword. On the far side of the yard lie the remains of buildings destroyed during World War II. These ruins serve a double purpose: they provide kids a place to hide when they play war games, and they provide folks privacy when they need to relieve themselves.

The east-facing edge of the court offers a panoramic view of *La Valle del Rapido*, the valley where the river that gives the town its name lazily winds its way westward to the *Mar Tirreno*. On the horizon, on top of its own mountain, looms *L'Abbazia di Montecassino*, the Benedictine monastery that adds historical significance to the region known as *La Ciociaria*. Because of its strategic location, the abbey has been destroyed and rebuilt several times since it was founded in 529 AD. Most recently, during the last war, it was blasted by the Allied Forces to gain access to Rome and liberate Italy. Subsequently, it has been rebuilt to its current grandeur.

I am proud to be from *Sant'Elia Fiumerapido* because we are close to Rome. As such, I consider myself a Roman citizen. When I play, I become a descendant of nobility, a centurion.

Mamma, Papà, and I live on the top floor of *Palazzo Gagliardi*. Our apartment has two rooms—one with a window, the other with a *balcone*. The room with the window is where *Mamma* cooks and we eat. I can only see the sky because I'm not allowed to stand on a chair to look out the window.

The room with the balcony is where we sleep and I play. *Mamma e Papà's* bed takes up most of the space. My cot is squished in the far corner, by the balcony. I play on the cement floor at the foot of my bed. From behind iron bars, I sometimes follow the movement of people on the street below as they go about their business. My mind often wanders, however. It goes to the edge of the courtyard, down by the river, across the valley, and over the mountains. Finally, it soars to the open sky, where I glide free.

It's summertime and school is out. I'm almost finished with my *zuppa di latte*. *Papà* drinks his *espresso* in one easy slurp and readies himself to leave. It must be close to 8:00 A.M., because that's when *Papà* goes to work. He can drink his coffee fast because he lets it cool down. Not like *Mamma*... she likes to drink her coffee scalding hot.

Mamma is already at work. She left early this morning when I was still asleep. She works at the paper factory. Far away. Even though it's my bicycle, *Mamma* uses it to go to work every day. At 4:00 P.M., when she comes back home, I'm allowed to ride it and go out to play.

I stand in the kitchen facing the door as *Papà* removes the key from the lock. The sound of his footsteps fades as he goes down the stairs. He'll be back at lunch, in four hours. I spend time alone in the apartment, waiting for *Mamma* or *Papà*.

I wish I were back in school. Last year, I learned about *Romolo*, the founder of Rome, and about *Ottaviano Augusto*, the founder of the Roman Empire. In class, *La Maestra* read many stories about ancient Rome. I like learning about the many heroes who helped shape the empire. I wish I had my textbook so I could read some more of those stories.

The only thing to read in our apartment is *Grand Hotel*, the weekly women's magazine that *Mamma* borrows from *Zia Ezia*, who lives on the ground floor. *Mamma* hides it from me because it has pictures I'm not supposed to see. But I know where it's hidden, on the top of the wardrobe. When I'm left alone, I climb onto a chair to retrieve it and flip through the pages. They are filled with pictures of men and women, sometimes kissing and sometimes in bed together, talking to each other through bubbles that cover up part of the image.

I like it best when others read. Last year, *La Maestra* asked me to read in front of the whole class. I couldn't do it. I sweated and I stuttered. And then she screamed at me. The following Sunday on her way to church, she stopped at *Papà*'s shop and told him what had happened. When *Papà* came home at lunchtime, he was angry with me. As punishment, he said I wouldn't be allowed to go to the *cinema* that afternoon. *Le Fatiche di Ercole* was playing, and I had been looking forward to seeing Hercules questing for the treasure of the Golden Fleece—so much so that I wished I hadn't stuttered.

I collect buttons. *Papà* gives them to me. He cuts them from old trousers and coats, and I use them as toy soldiers when I recreate battle scenes between the Romans and their enemies. Sometimes I go with *Papà* to the shop, and when it's not busy, he lets me play on the big table at the back. I can play with as many shiny new buttons as I want, as long as I don't lose them. I start by grouping the buttons according to size, shape, and color. The small buttons are foot soldiers. The fewer larger buttons are commanders. I have a favorite button, one of a kind. It's not round like all the others but square. And it is not one color but a combination. It's like a mini picture frame with gold corners. He's the most dependable, the most courageous of all Romans. He is a centurion and always wins. He is everything I wish I could be.

Views from the Balcony

The Abbey of *Montecassino* on the hilltop as seen from parents' home

Beyond the Rapido Valley - *Monte Cifalco* in the distance

CHAPTER 4

Rigatoni al Sugo di Carne
Pasta with Meat Sauce

I OPEN THE BALCONY DOOR AND THE NOISE FROM OUTSIDE FILLS the bedroom. The market is in full swing. I sit on the platform with my legs crossed and my back wedged in the outside corner against the railing. I face the valley. My army is assembling on this side of the river. On the other side is the enemy. Both armies are ready for battle. The centurion, his golden helmet reflecting the rays of the sun, is perched on my knee, a hilltop, assessing the battle scene. He and I inspect our legions—row upon row of regimented soldiers. We are proud and sure to win. As for the enemy, their camp is bedlam. Men in partial armor scramble between tents searching for weapons. Others, bare-chested, run around brandishing their swords in the air aimlessly.

In the courtyard below, a chaotic scene unfolds. People move frantically about. A woman enters a shop, another exits. One stops to greet, another rushes by. One offers a price, another reacts in shock. Voices get louder and louder. The screech of a vendor rises above the din: "*Venite qua, signò, per la verdura più fresca! E a buonissimo prezzo!*" Look here, ladies, for the freshest greens! And at the best price!

A twitch in my leg is followed by a kick. One of my soldiers slides towards the edge. Immediately, I'm on a fast gallop to his rescue. I return him safely to his ranks and receive shouts of praise from my army. The shouts continue, but now they come from a different direction… from the street below. They're no longer accolades, but cries for attention. The row of vendors is my Roman line of defense, and the sporadic movement of the townspeople is the advancing enemy. The confrontation of buyer and seller is the clash of the Roman sword against the enemy's shield. The battle rages on.

The shoppers have gone home. Exhausted, the vendors shake out the discarded leafage to the ground and throw the empty wicker baskets back onto the carts, while the donkeys nervously shift back and forth. In the quietude, I hear the crunching of stones under wagons loaded with the wounded. The screeching of rolling wheels. The snapping of whips. The neighing of mules. The thunder of marching soldiers. I see all this from atop.

Within my armor, I feel the vibrations. The red plumage of my helmet bounces up and down as I trot. Up ahead, I notice a little boy standing tiptoe on the front step of a portal. That of *Palazzo Gagliardi*. I approach, lean to the left, and offer the boy my arm. He takes it, and I scoop him up behind me on the saddle. As I do, I hear shouts of approval from my men. The boy tightens his hold around my waist. Buoyed by the cheers, we gallop ahead. I detect a familiar sound among the shouts. *Papà?* It's our unique whistle signal. I see him standing there, outside his shop at the top of the street, so I jump off my horse and stand up. I grab two iron bars to pull myself up above the top railing and return his signal with a wave of my arm. He points to his wristwatch to indicate that it's time. I nod in return and quickly head for the kitchen.

At the stove, I turn the burner under the large pot fully on and the burner under the small pot halfway on. Last night, before I went to bed, *Mamma* showed me what to do. The big pot is almost full of water, and the small pot contains the leftover sauce from yesterday. On most Sundays, *Mamma* makes meat sauce. Sometimes there's sauce left over, but never any meat. The next step is to set the table for just me and *Papà*. *Mamma* doesn't come home for lunch because she works far away. From the cupboard, I take two flat plates, two bowls, and two glasses and arrange them on the table. From the drawer, two forks; I remember no spoons today because we're having *pasta asciutta*. From the tap, I fill my glass with water and place it by my plate. From the countertop beside the stove, I take the half-full bottle of red wine and place it near *Papà's* glass. I look around and locate the covered bowl that *Mamma* said not to forget. I know what's in it, so I place it on *Papà's* side, away from me, hoping he won't make me eat it, because I don't like *rapini*. With everything done, I run back to the balcony.

The buttons are all mixed together. I gather them in my cloth bag for future battles. The *piazza* is much quieter. It's empty except for a stray dog rummaging through the trash left behind by the vendors. *Peppino*, the street cleaner, will sweep it all up later in the afternoon. The bells of *La Chiesa Madre* announce the time: *miéziuórn* (twelve noon). As if waiting for a signal, '*Ndònih gliu scarpar* (*Antonio* the cobbler) darts out of his shop, locks the door, and walks away. A few moments later, *Papà* emerges from his shop and locks up. Instead of walking down towards me, he runs across the street and disappears into *Marietta's* bakery shop. It takes forever for him to come out. When he finally does, he's holding a loaf of bread under his arm. He walks very fast and soon disappears under me. I go back to the kitchen and stand in front of the door, waiting. I hear *Papà* whistling as he comes up the stairs. I think he's skipping every other step because he sounds close. The key is in the lock, a click, and *Papà* suddenly appears.

The lids on the pots make a clapping sound. *Papà* puts the loaf of bread on the table and rushes to the stove. He lifts the cover of the small pot and stirs the sauce. The aroma fills the room and suddenly I feel very hungry. He then removes the cover from the large pot and drops the *rigatoni* in the boiling water. My mouth is full of saliva. I swallow, but more saliva comes. I am starving! I sit at my place and tear an end piece from the loaf. It's warm. I take a bite and chew. My eyes remain fixed on *Papà*. By the sink, he drains the pasta in the colander and dumps it back in the pot. He then adds the sauce to it and stirs while he brings the steaming container to the table. I hold my fork firmly in my right hand and close my eyes… I am the centurion. I hold my sword firmly in my right hand and take a deep breath. My lungs fill with the sweet aroma… my soldiers wait for the signal… I open my eyes and see the steaming mount of pasta. *Papà* says, "*Magna, Bru, magna*" (eat, Bruno, eat), as he too sits down to eat. I stab one then two pieces of *rigatoni* and close my eyes again… my sword is high above my head… my mouth opens. I take a bite and close my eyes. The signal? No! Later! Now, it is time to eat!

2011 – The 4th floor balcony of *Palazzo Gagliardi* as seen from *Papà's* tailor shop
(with *Papà* in the foreground … retracing the steps of long ago)

CHAPTER 5

La Bottiglia Scivolosa
The Slippery Bottle

I AM ON THE BATTLEFIELD. MY HORSE RAISES BOTH FRONT LEGS and squeals. I pull back and hold on tight. I lift my hands to protect my head. I fall down…

I am six years old. *Mamma* gives me a beating. *"Ma pcché? Pcché? Pcché?"* Why do you have to hurt me so? Why can't you just for once do as I say? Why am I forever being punished? *"Povera disgraziata che song!"* Poor retched soul that I am! Then, with sorrowful eyes, she looks at me and begs for forgiveness. "Why did you make me hurt you so?"

I am in second grade. Not pleased, *La Maestra* points her finger at me. "Your father will be none too happy when he hears about this!"

I am an altar boy. From behind the confessional grill, *Don Mario* threatens me: "Hell is where all sinners go!"

I am *maleducato* (ill-mannered/rude). *Papà*'s callused hand smacks the back of my head. "This will teach you not to talk back!"

Voices surround me. They become arrows. Arrowhead after arrowhead reaches its target. The shield I hold is my protection.

27

I feel safe... to a point. I will myself to become small. And smaller. Almost invisible. I must be strong. I hold on. I endure.

"Take this, you scoundrel!"

"Not another word from you!"

"Sit down!"

"No talking back, you wretch!"

La Maestra is my elementary schoolteacher from Grade 1 through to Grade 5. She is very strict and mean. She always wears her black hair tied tightly back into a bun. A dark moustache covers her upper lip, and hair grows on a big mole on her left cheek. Her voice is raspy and high-pitched. She reminds me of a witch. And I am afraid of her. I'm most afraid when she threatens to tell *Papà* about my bad behavior in class.

I look out the window and my mind wanders. *La Maestra* always catches me. On my report cards she notes: "Bruno is easily distracted." On Sunday mornings, after mass, she often stops by *Papà*'s shop and reports on my progress or lack thereof. In return, *Papà* offers to fix her son's trousers *gratis*, for free. After she leaves, *Papà* berates me in front of all the people in the shop. I feel ashamed.

"*Disgraziato!*" (Unfortunate!)

"Don't touch it!"

"How many times have you been told to walk away?"

"*Povera a mè!*" (Poor me!)

"Come here, I'll give you reason to cry!"

"After all we do for you. To what end? Eh?"

"And this is how you pay us back?"

"*Mannaggia quant so' nata!*" (Damn the day I was born!)

All is quiet now. The enemy appears to have withdrawn. I

hear a gentle snorting. I turn my head and open my eyes to take a peek from the edge of my shield. My horse stands tall beside me and greets me with a nicker. He paws his foreleg to indicate that he's been waiting. I get up. He raises his tail in excitement.

There is no running water in our apartment. To cook, clean, and wash, *Mamma* gets water from the fountain in the courtyard across the *Palazzo Gagliardi*. She fills *la cannata* and *il bottiglione* with fresh water. *La cannata*, the three-gallon terracotta vessel, is for cleaning and washing. *Il bottiglione*, the two-liter glass bottle, is for drinking and cooking. Normally *Mamma* goes to the fountain twice each day, once in the morning and once in the afternoon. She is very strong. She can carry both containers full of water at the same time. She places *la spara*, the donut-shaped roll that she made from old rags, on the flat of her head and lifts *la cannata* from the ground onto *la spara*. When she feels the load is balanced, she grabs *il bottiglione* with her left hand and begins the trek across the courtyard to the *palazzo*, up the eighty-eight stairs to our apartment. Once inside, *Mamma* places *il bottiglione* on the table and then finally raises *la cannata* off her head onto the countertop in the corner of the kitchen. A couple of times I have tried to lift *la cannata* when it was empty, but I couldn't do it.

Palazzo Gagliardi is a very old building. *Mamma e Papà* rent a two-room apartment on the top floor. They moved here when I was almost three years old, before my sister *Fulvia* was born. There are three apartments on the fourth floor; ours is the middle one. The one on the right belongs to *D'virata*. The one on the left belongs to *Marisa e Antonio*. *D'virata* lives alone and keeps mostly to herself. *Marisa e Antonio* have four daughters:

the twins, *Renata e Vera*, and *Wilma* and *Orietta*. The twins are the oldest, about the same age as *Fulvia*. *Fulvia* often plays with the four sisters. Sometimes I'm allowed to join them. But being the oldest and a boy, *Marisa* hovers close by to supervise. The scantily lit fourth-floor landing is where the six of us usually play.

The zigzag stairway that connects the four floors is lit with a lone bare incandescent bulb that hangs at the center of each landing. When a bulb burns out, it doesn't get replaced right away. Usually it takes an accident. Not long ago, *Orietta*, *Marisa*'s youngest daughter, slipped through a space in the iron railing where a spindle had been missing. She fell from the third floor down to the stone steps on the ground floor. Not yet two years old, she survived the drop with hardly a bruise to show. Some say it was the bouncing from side to side that broke the impact of the fall. Others say that it was the parachute effect of the little dress she wore. All agreed that it was a miracle. Since then, light bulbs have been replaced promptly. Well… almost. And the gap in the fence has been remedied by weaving a metal cord from spindle to spindle.

It is *ora di pranzo*, lunchtime. *Il bottiglione* is empty because *Mamma* didn't have time to go to the fountain today. This morning, she and *Papà* were screaming at each other. I don't know why. But *Mamma* has been stewing all morning. She asked *Papà* to bring a bottle of water on his way home, but he forgot. She fumes. He responds to her rage by yelling and cursing. She doesn't give in but tells him to keep his voice down. "The neighbors don't need to know our business," she says. This makes *Papà* raise his voice even more. "Send your son down to the fountain, for Christ's sake!" he shouts. Hoping to stifle their anger somewhat, I am ready to go.

Mamma takes an empty one-liter bottle from the cupboard and tells me to "be careful." I wrap my right hand firmly around the neck of the bottle and proceed down the staircase, one step at a time. It is dark. To keep my balance, I hold-on to the railing with my left hand while, with my thumb, I count the passing spindles waiting for the spot where one is missing, where *Orietta* fell through. I reach the first corner... my eyes are closed... it is night... I become *Muzio Scevola*... I am at the edge of the encampment... it's hard to make out any shapes... I tighten the grip on my sword... slowly, I advance in search of a place to enter the enemy camp... it's close, I feel it... suddenly, a loud blast... glass smashing on a stone surface... I squeeze my right hand but... it's empty?!... the sword?!... the bottle?!

Mamma's screeching replaces the shattering noise. I look up to the railing outside our door to realize that I have barely made it to the second floor. Instantly, *Mamma* is next to me with the broom and dustbin. She hits me over the head with the broomstick but not with full force. It's as if she changes her mind halfway through the motion. Back upstairs, *Papà* sits at the table eating and drinking, alone. In between mouthfuls, he barks nasty comments directed mostly at *Mamma*.

I'm going down the stairs again, with another bottle. Holding back tears, I concentrate on what I'm doing. I reach the fountain without incident. Before filling the bottle, I rinse it. I hold it by the neck tightly with my right hand and use my left hand to push down the fountain tap to open the water flow. I fill it with just enough water to swish it inside to remove any dirt and sediment. I repeat the action one more time. Ready to fill the bottle, I hold it as close to the tap as I can to fill it faster. At the halfway point, I sense the bottle sliding down inside my fist. I strengthen my grip, but the slip continues. My arm starts to ache and I panic. The bottle gets heavier. It escapes my hold and crashes to the ground with a muffled burst. Shards of glass and cold water hit my bare legs.

"*Bruno!*" *Mamma* screams from the kitchen window. It's as if she's calling me from the heavens. Bewildered and with empty hands, I run back to the apartment. *Mamma* and I practically fall into one another on the first floor. How did she get here so fast? Instead of a comforting hug, she pounds her clenched fists on my head. I accept her punishment and hold back any resistance. She grabs me by the arm and pulls me up the stairs. From his chair, *Papà* spews more venom, but I don't hear him, nor do I register the ongoing mayhem between him and *Mamma*. I am sent to the fountain one more time. This time I succeed. After rinsing the bottle, I place it on the ground in line with the water stream. Holding it with both hands, I lift the full bottle and carry it home.

My achievement stands in the middle of the table like a prized trophy. But there is no claimant. *Papà* stares at the empty plate in front of him and sips what remains of his wine. *Mamma*, her back to us, stands at the sink and scrubs a pot she used to prepare the meal. Her plate on the table is barely touched. I am hungry but unable to move my arm to bring a forkful to my mouth. The silence is disturbing.

My horse nickers as I straighten my centurion uniform and tighten my helmet. I check the girth before I mount him again. I sink into the saddle and push into a gallop towards the legions that await inspection. Tomorrow we will face the enemy one more time.

1960s – The Fountain

CHAPTER 6
Pasta e Baccalà
Pasta with Salted Cod

LA MAESTRA NODS HER HEAD AS A SIGN FOR ME TO BEGIN READING:
"*Volevo uccidere te. La mia mano ha errato e ora la punisco per questo imperdonabile errore.' Così mise la sua mano destra in un braciere dove ardeva il fuoco dei sacrifici e non la tolse fino a che non fu completamente consumata.*" ("I wanted to kill you. My hand has erred and now I punish it for this unforgivable mistake." So he placed his right hand in a brazier where the fire of sacrifices burned and did not remove it until it was completely consumed.) This time I don't stutter, and my voice doesn't quaver. Last night, I read this same passage over and over again until I had it memorized. I stand in front of the class and make it look like I'm reading, but I'm not. *La Maestra* is pleased. When I finish, she says, "*Bravo, Bruno. Bravo.*"

I like the story of *Muzio Scevola*. He is the most courageous of all Romans. When Rome is under siege from the Etruscans, he takes it upon himself to infiltrate the enemy camp and kill their king. Unfortunately, he's caught before he can complete his mission. When brought to face the king, he notices a fiery canister nearby. Without hesitation, he sidesteps towards it and

35

thrusts his right hand deep into the burning coals. He holds it there until it is consumed. I imagine the pain he must have felt, and I shudder. Impressed by such bravery, the Etruscan king decides to end the encirclement of Rome and returns to his homeland. In conclusion, by sacrificing his hand, *Muzio Scevola* attains his goal and becomes a hero!

"*Bravo, Bruno. Bravo*" resonates in my head as I walk home. I am so eager to share my success with *Mamma e Papà* that I forget what day it is. But as soon as I enter the portal of *Palazzo Gagliardi*, I remember. I smell *baccalà*. It's Friday!

I wish I was *Muzio Scevola*, or just had a little of his courage. Because of me, *Mamma e Papà* are upset. Because of me, *Mamma* is crying. Because of me, *Papà* is back at work, angry. And because of me, everyone in the building knows our business. It's all my fault because I didn't eat my *pasta e baccalà!*

Most Fridays, *Mamma* makes *pasta e baccalà*. The only variable is the shape of pasta she uses. Today, for example, she chose to cook *tubetti*—stubby little tubes that tend to fill up with the scolding sauce. I burn my palate every time. The tomato-based gravy contains chunks of *baccalà*, the salted cod that stinks up the whole building when *Mamma* starts to soak it, usually the night before. I repeatedly tell *Mamma* that I don't like the taste and the smell of *baccalà*, but she says, "It's the only fish I can afford to buy with the pittance your father gives me!"

Papà sits at the head of the table, facing the window. He slurps steaming spoonfuls of *baccalà* noisily into his mouth. *Mamma* is to his left, close to the stove. She makes no sound except when she swallows. I'm on *Papà*'s right, near the fireplace, frozen in my chair and facing my hot bowl.

"*Bru, magna*" (Bruno, eat), *Mamma* urges me.

My forearms rest heavy on the table. I hold my spoon tightly in my right fist, unable to move. Inside my head, I see *Muzio Scevola* on top of a hill. He assesses the enemy camp below. I gauge the bowl through a fog. *Muzio* acts without fear. All he has is a dagger. My hand squeezes the spoon. What am I afraid of? Surely not the *baccalà?*

"*Bru, magna,*" *Mamma* begs. Her words break my spell, but I remain immobile. To finish off, *Mamma e Papà* use chunks of bread to soak up the remaining gravy, leaving their dish so clean that they won't require washing.

"*Bru, magna. P' piàcere. Nh mh 'fa 'ncazzà.*" (Bruno, eat. Please. Don't make me angry.) *Papà* pipes in. I summon all my strength and focus my attention on the surface of my dish. The *tubetti* stare back at me. They taunt me with their fill of unsavory *baccalà*. My arm lifts off the tabletop. With the tip of the spoon, I sweep across and catch two tubes. Carefully, I drag them across to the edge of the plate and tap them to clear the cavities of any filling. Using the slant of the rim to my advantage, I trap the pasta onto the spoon. I hold my breath and open my mouth as I lift the loaded spoon to my lips. Reluctantly, I accept the catch. I grimace as my taste buds confirm the failed scraping efforts—the taste of *baccalà* persists. I chew but cannot swallow. The back of my throat is sealed shut.

Mamma e Papà have moved on to the next course that is doubly offensive to me: *baccalà e verdura*. After *baccalà*, I hate *verdura*. I don't like its bitter taste! They eat in silence, and I sense their exasperation building. To end the meal, *Mamma* brings out a wedge of *provolone* and half-a-loaf of fresh bread. My mouth waters at the sight. I wish I could sink my teeth into the bread, but I taste the mush I hold in my mouth instead. And I almost swallow!

"*Bru, magna,*" *Mamma* pleads for the umpteenth time.

I remain a solid block. Unresponsive. Suddenly, *Papà* explodes by cursing the day I was born. By blaspheming all the saints, the Virgin, Jesus Christ, and even his own namesake, Saint Rocco, for the day he married and the burden he now carries. He pounds his fist on the table as if to punctuate his declaration. Plates, glasses, and cutlery bounce up and fall noisily back down. He gets up and pushes his chair against the table. It crashes to the ground. The door slams shut behind him.

I'm not sure how it all started, but that's how it ended. And it's all my fault because I refused to eat even one morsel. And now *Mamma* is sad. *Papà* is angry. My mouth is full of mush that I can't swallow or spit out. If I do spit out, *Mamma* will be more upset. She has put *Papà*'s chair upright and has cleared the table, except for my bowl. She now stands at the sink doing the dishes. She continues to sulk. I hear her sniveling.

I stare at the cold *tubetti e baccalà*… in the translucent tomato sauce…

the tomatoes are burning coals in a canister… I am *Muzio Scevola*… my goal: to free Rome… make *Mamma* happy. I have broken through the enemy line… I am one step closer to killing the king… the guards have seen me… they catch up with me… they bring me to their king… I have failed… I must be punished… I am not worthy to be a son… what is that? The fire of sacrifice? Yes, that is my punishment… the eyes of the king are on me… the intense heat awaits… our eyes lock… my hand plunges into the flame… hold it… hold it…

"Bruno!" *Mamma* shrieks.

I snap out of my trance. My right hand is deep into the plate of *tubetti e baccalà*. The mixture has splattered all over the table-cloth. The shriek lands a sharp slap across the back of my head.

The plate is snatched and disappears in the sink with a clank. Another slap follows. The tablecloth is gathered and pulled away. *Mamma*'s shrieks fill the room. She screams. Lashes out at me with closed fists. Pounds my head... yes, hit me... harder... I must be punished... for I have failed... I must pay... I can endure the pain... yes, I can... am I not, *Muzio Scevola, cittadino di Roma?!*

Main Entrance to *Palazzo Gagliardi*   Descent to *Nonna*'s house

CHAPTER 7

Zio Ettore
Uncle Hector

THE STONES I WALK ON REFLECT THE HEAT UP MY BARE LEGS AS the bright sun beats down over my head. Beads of sweat run like tears down my forehead. The salt makes my eyes sting. I rub them with my free hand, but it makes it worse. In my right hand I carry a wicker bag, the lunch I didn't eat. I stretch out my arm as far as I can. I hold my breath and twitch my nose, but I can still smell the *baccalà*.

"*Nonna*'s chickens will feast on it!" *Mamma* said.

Nonna lives in the outskirts of the village in a housing complex called *Le Telare*, across from the old paper mill, *La Cartiera*. It's a long way to her apartment. I walk along *Via Angelo Santilli* and go past *La Chiesa Madre*, where I am an altar boy. I pass by *La Cantina di Panzone*, where I come to buy a half-liter of wine for *Papà*. About halfway there, I reach *Fuori San Cataldo*, a *piazzetta* outside what used to be the eastern portal of *San Cataldo*. I stop at the water fountain and place the bag flat on the ground, making sure that the contents don't spill. I cup my hands and fill them with cold water. I drink from the cup. Then I refill and splash the water on my face to cool down.

From this vantage point, I can see the valley below, the *Fiume Rapido* and *Le Telare*. Where *Via Angelo Santilli* ends, there are ruins of the gated entryway of long ago. *Nonna* remembers these portals. She tells of how the people of *Sant'Elia* built a wall around the village as protection against thieves and bandits. To get in and out of the village, they placed large stone portals at strategic places along the perimeter of the wall. One such portal is where I now stand: *La Porta di San Cataldo*. I imagine myself as a guard at this entryway... I must remain alert. My people depend on me! With this thought, I pick up the stinky sack with my left hand and begin *la discesa della Cartiera* (the descent towards the old paper mill), the steep roadway that leads down to a bridge over the *Fiume Rapido* and onto the large square. *Le Telare* is directly across, adjacent to the river.

Nonna's apartment is on the second floor, at the end of a long dark hallway. I knock and soon I hear muffled steps on the other side. *Nonna* opens the door and greets me with a big toothless smile. I lift my arm holding the heavy bag, and she immediately takes it from me with little effort.

"*Hmmm... ché bella puzza r' baccalà!*" What a nice stench of *baccalà*, she says. And turns around and walks across the kitchen to the large bay window that overlooks the yard. She places the bag on the sill, takes the covered dish out, lifts the screen, and calls her chickens over: "*Beeeeeh... peeh... peeh... beeh... beeeeeeh...*"

I stand on my tiptoes beside her as she dumps the contents of the dish down below. The chickens scurry over, peck at the scraps of food, and dash a safe distance away to enjoy the treat. I look for the white rooster. I see him. In no hurry, he struts over to inspect the offering. As he prances forward, the hens make way. Undisturbed, he jabs chunks of the *pasta e baccalà*. He extends his white neck and projects his golden beak forward. He stiffens his crimson crest... I straddle my horse. From the hilltop, I observe my men as they chase away the last of the enemy forces.

Satisfied, I guide the white mare down the incline. My helmet shines in the sunlight. The red crest waves from side to side...

"*Bru, t tèh fam?*" (Bruno, are you hungry?) *Nonna* asks.

I snap out of my trance and nod yes.

"*Assiett't allora.*" (Sit down then.) She points to the chair at one end of the kitchen table.

I sit as directed while she darts about her tiny kitchen like a bee in a bottle. From the cupboard, she takes a half loaf of bread and cuts two thick slices. Returns the loaf to the cupboard. Places the slices on a plate. She forks a *cotoletta di pollo* from a covered dish on the counter and places it on one slice and covers it with the other. From the same counter, she retrieves a bowl of leftover tomato salad. She holds the sandwich in one hand, and the salad in the other. She turns and places both—plate and bowl—in front of me. Completes the turn and she's at the sink. Returns to me with a glass of water.

"*Magna Bru, magna. Ch na' bona saluta.*" (Eat, Bruno, eat. To your good health.)

I grab the sandwich with both hands and eat hungrily. When I'm done, she takes the empty plate away. I get the hiccups.

"*Bivh l'acqua*" (Drink water), she tells me.

I turn my attention to the tomato salad and proceed to stab each wedge with my fork. Secured, I transfer the slippery catch into my open mouth. In the meantime, *Nonna* has cut another slice of bread.

"*Affun'la a luogl*" (Soak it in the oil), she says.

I soak up the oil and garlic and leave the dish spotless.

"*Vuo 'na bella mela?*" (Do you want a nice apple?) she asks.

I'm about to burst. I shake my head and refuse the apple.

Satisfied, *Nonna* tells me to go rest in the next room while she cleans up. She cautions me to be quiet because *Zio Ettore* may be snoozing. All this time, I didn't know that *Zio Ettore* was next door.

I like *Zio Ettore*. He's the youngest of all my uncles and he rides a *Vespa*. Sometimes he takes me for a ride. He goes very fast and tells me to hold on tight. I too want a *Vespa* when I grow up. I open the door quietly. *Zio Ettore* is awake. He sits in one of the padded chairs in the far corner and looks up from a magazine to welcome me. *"Ciao Brunello, come stai?"* (Hi Bruno, how are you?) And returns to flipping pages.

"Bene, grazie" (Well, thank you), I reply timidly as I enter the room and close the door behind me. My tummy is extra full. I wish I could sit on one of those comfy chairs, but *Zio Ettore* is there and I mustn't disturb him. So I cross the room and go stand at the window that overlooks the other side of the yard. The sun is bright. I hear the muffled clucking of the hens as they graze the grass. And I hear the sound of running water at the far side of the garden. This gentle sound mix is suddenly broken up by a loud crowing as my favorite white rooster announces his presence. The red crest shines in the sunlight, like a beacon. He stands alone. Fearful, the hens keep a distance. He pecks the ground and jerkily looks around as if he too, is afraid. Of what? I wonder… as I drift onto the battlefield … I am on my white mare. We prance over the carnage. My men scuttle about snuffing out any sign of life…

I hear movement behind me. Is *Zio Ettore* going? He clears his throat. He takes a step, then another. A deep inhale. Another step. He is coming towards me. I want to turn around but I can't. Instead, I stare at the yard in front of me. Another step. Then, no more. He is right behind me. I feel his breath on the back of my neck. I tense. I feel his body touch my behind. He inches a little closer. Pushes me forward. My hips hit the wall. Then he pulls back and pushes forward again. I hold my breath. I feel something hard pressing against my bottom. He pushes against me. Back and forth. Harder. Faster. I want him to stop. *Nonna. Mamma. Papà.* Help me! But I have no voice. And I must endure… because I am a centurion… from the hilltop I assess the legions… they are well-rested and well-fed… they are ready for battle... we will win... I will lead them to victory!

Behind me, the front door slams shut. In front of me, the rooster crows. In the kitchen, *Nonna* snores. I turn around. The door is wide open. No sign of *Zio Ettore*. Outside, the sound of a scooter. Vroom... vroom. I turn around. I recognize *Zio Ettore* on his *Vespa*. His left foot kicks the release of the stand. Vroom... vroom. He speeds away, leaving nothing but a trail of smoke.

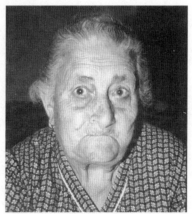

1970s – *Nonna*

CHAPTER 8

Maleducato

Bad Education

IF I WERE A HOUSE, *MAMMA E PAPÀ* WOULD HAVE SET THE FOUN-
dation, *La Maestra* and *Don Mario* would have built the walls,
and my friends would have provided the doors and windows.
From the moment I was born, *Mamma e Papà* kept my wings
well clipped and my leash so short that I couldn't fall or be
tempted to fly. Elementary school curriculum and public cat-
echism solidified my parents' controlling principles with their
stifling indoctrination. The bricks they used—an endless supply
of Hail Marys and Our Fathers—were made of fear and eternal
damnation. Luckily, I had friends. From them, I learned to
dream... not about a blissful afterlife, but rather to aspire to
new heights.

Whenever I complained, *Mamma e Papà* would begin their lam-
entation. When they were my age, they didn't have a pot to piss
in. They were refugees in their own country. Without a roof over
their heads. Rags for clothes. Starved most of the time. Had to be
content with a chunk of moldy bread. And did they complain?

Of course not. Besides, what could their poor mothers do with seven other hungry mouths to feed? And yet here I was with a warm, dry place to live, a soft bed to sleep in, comfortable clothes to wear, and hot food three times a day, going to school, to church... and still complaining? *La rascia è 'na brutta bestia!* Abundance is an ugly beast, they would conclude.

Our apartment was warm and cozy, especially if the fireplace was on. And I could look up at the window in the kitchen and see the sky. Through the iron railing on the balcony, I could see townspeople shopping in the courtyard below, and farmers plowing their fields in the valley.

In the classroom, *La Maestra* didn't like it when she caught me looking out the window. She would yell out my name and tell me to stop daydreaming and to pay attention instead. In my report card, she summarized my recurring behavior with a curt admonishment: Bruno is easily distracted.

I was an altar boy. In the confession booth, *Don Mario* promised me a bright future, but only if I repented of my sins and followed the examples set by Jesus Christ, the Virgin Mary, his disciples, and all the saints. He reaffirmed God's omnipotence and supreme knowledge. And that there was no place to hide. Only by following his path would I be assured a place in heaven. An eternal peaceful existence where I floated on puffy white clouds all day, my face caressed by the wings of angels.

In my heart I held a secret. I didn't want the same life as *Mamma e Papà*. I didn't want to be confined in the tiny class-room. And I didn't want to die to live eternally. In my mind, I escaped these boundaries at every opportunity. My imagination gave me freedom. I soared in the sky beyond the kitchen window. I galloped over the mountains surrounding the village to foreign lands. I ventured into magical forests through the trees in the schoolyard. And I broke through the grate of the confessional to enter a world full of other possibilities. This was where I wanted to be. This was my dream. My secret.

Mamma e Papà? Why bother them? What more could they offer me? They were powerless. *La Maestra?* As far as I was concerned, she could keep adding notes to my report cards all she liked. What would they change? And *Don Mario?* Well, I couldn't let him in on my secret, but if he wanted to know the truth, he knew whom to ask, did he not?

From kindergarten through to Grade 8, I was among the youngest and the shortest in the class. None of my classmates lived or played near my home. Consequently, my free time was spent with boys who were older than me. And being short meant that I almost went unnoticed.

Amongst these older boys were my two cousins, *Roberto* and *Carminuccio*, who were three-and-a-half and two-and-a-half years older, respectively. Then there were the four boys who lived near *Palazzo Gagliardi. Bruno* and *Felicetto* lived in the building across from me, and *Franco* and *Tommasino* lived next door. With the exception of *Tommasino*, they were all older than me by at least a year. And near *Papà's* shop, where I spent a lot of time, was the cobbler's son, *Paoletto*, who was two-and-a-half-years older, and *Germano*, the apprentice, who was almost twice my age.

Each year of my adolescence, from October to June, I spent the mornings in a conventional classroom. The rest of the time, I studied in an alternate classroom where I learned differently. In this parallel education, attendance was not mandatory but enticing. Report cards weren't issued. Parental involvement was not required. In fact, it was discouraged. Here, the teachings were sworn secrets. Unknowingly, I had become a member of a clandestine boys' club that rebelled against authority. In public, I may have seemed the saintly altar boy, but I was becoming a sinful rioter. This burgeoning dual personality simultaneously scared and excited me.

It was in this furtive environment that *Roberto* taught me how to make a pseudo-cigarette. In alleyways, we collected tobacco from discarded butts. Then we tore strips from old newspapers and rolled the rancid collection into a smokable facsimile. It was *Carminuccio* who later showed me how to inhale the putrid creation. But I could never bring myself to smoke it. Amongst ruins I learned about sex. It began with *Germano* giving me a crash course in masturbation. I remained shocked for a while, but in time and with help from other boys, I began to assimilate the lesson. It didn't take long before I became an avid practitioner. *Franco* was proud of his emerging pubic hair, and he pulled me aside one day to show it to me. I felt envious because I had a long wait ahead of me. Collectively, these club members taught me how to objectify the opposite sex. To evaluate each body part as if it was a separate entity. The breast. The bottom. The leg. The mouth. From pictures of naked women, I began to understand desire. That certain type of craving. The hunger to conquer. To overcome. To escape.

When I'm too sick to go to school, I stay home in bed and *Mamma* misses a day or two of work. To take my temperature, she places the glass thermometer under my tongue and directs me to close my mouth around it without moving the stick, and to remain still. At 38.2 degrees Celsius, I have a fever. She straightens the blankets that cover me and tells me to sleep. When I wake up, I'm soaked to the bone with sweat. Exasperated, she changes the sheets for dry ones and helps me replace my wet undershirt and pajamas. She measures my temperature one more time. It's slightly higher than before. She goes to the doctor's office, and I fall asleep. When the doctor arrives, he conducts a quick assessment of my condition and prescribes a cure. Usually it comprises a series of daily injections that span a week, sometimes two. Relieved, *Mamma* tucks me in tightly and tells me to sleep. She goes to the pharmacy for the medicine. On her way back, she stops in the courtyard below *Palazzo Gagliardi* and calls up to *Maria*, the nurse. She lives on the top floor of the building across from us. *Mamma* asks her to give me my first injection.

I don't like needles because I can't relax. As soon as I feel the prick on my buttock, I tense up. That makes the muscle sore to sit on. But I don't mind because when I go by myself to *Maria's* apartment to get the remaining shots, I am sometimes invited to stay and play with her son, *Bruno*. He's just a little older than me and has two brothers, one older and one younger, and a baby sister. They have lots of different toys that they share with me. *Bruno* also has a television. If I'm lucky, I go for my shot when *Le Avventure di Rin-Tin-Tin* is on TV. *Maria* lets me stay and watch the show with her kids, and I forget about the pain in my buttock. I like how the boy named Rusty and his dog, Rin-Tin-Tin, help the soldiers maintain law and order in the Wild West. I wish *Mamma e Papà* had a TV so I could continue to follow Rusty's adventures. I also wish I could have a friend like Rin-Tin-Tin. I hear *Mamma's* voice from our kitchen window shouting across the yard. She says that it's time for me to come home. She apologizes for the trouble I caused. *Maria* reassures her that I am a very well-behaved boy and am welcome anytime. She tells *Mamma* that I'm watching TV and that the program will be over soon.

I am home. *Mamma* is upset. I feel anxious. She doesn't scold me directly, but I sense that she's angry with me. I know why. I have burdened her with yet another job. She has to make a cake or something for *Maria*. For her troubles. And it's all because of me. Why could I not just have gotten my shot and come straight home?

❊

Mamma repeatedly warns me not to play in team sports and to stay away from those other boys. She says I can get hurt because I'm smaller than them. And younger. And because they play too rough. She is right, of course. Not that long ago, I disobeyed her and participated in a soccer game in the courtyard in front of *Palazzo Gagliardi*. At first, I had refused. But the group had insisted. They needed an eighth player to make the two teams even. It was just a friendly little game. A simple back-and-forth tossing of the ball. That's all. Nothing rough. I really wanted to play, so I shut off *Mamma's* voice in my head and joined them.

At first, I stayed away from pursuing the ball to avoid confrontation with another player, but as I warmed up in competition, my fear melted away and I became bolder in my actions. I challenged myself. I controlled the ball briefly. I even kicked at the net. My first kick was too soft, and the goalie caught the ball without difficulty. I felt invigorated and empowered, and I began to enjoy the feeling when someone kicked the ball very high. I followed its trajectory up and then down. It was coming towards me. No doubt this would be my first header. A rush of adrenaline. My eyes remained fixed on the ball as my forehead readied to meet it. I inhaled deeply, bent my knees, and sprung my body upwards, aiming for the net. My intent was to score. I jumped. And I collided. But in a three-way encounter. The top of *Felicetto's* head met the ball, and his forehead met the edge of my right eyebrow. I fell to the ground. My hand to my eye… throbbing pain… blood… confusion… fear… more pain… voices calling… *Bruno*… *Mamma*… more fear… more confusion… screams… blood flowing down my face and hand… to my shirt… *Mamma* beside me… reproaching… crying… cursing… regrets… more fear.

A couple of hours pass. *Mamma* and I are back in the apartment. She is silent and sad. The pain in my brow is numb. A white dressing covers most of my right eye. We have been to the doctor. I required stitches. Three. I will have a scar, he said.

It will take weeks to heal. My first ever scar. A badge of honor? What will the boys think? But *Mamma* was right. I should not play in team sports. I promise to never play in team sports again. The scar will be my reminder!

Tommasino e Franco are the pharmacist's sons. They live in the building next door. A narrow path that leads to the river separates the two buildings. Halfway down, there are the remnants of a building destroyed during the war. The ruins can be seen from the edge of the courtyard on the other side of *Palazzo Gagliardi*. The outline of the rooms is traceable by the partial walls that still stand. They are overgrown with thick, thorny blackberry bushes.

When the two brothers come out to play, I join them. In the courtyard, we pass the ball around. Initially, we're a couple of feet apart and our kicks are slow and soft. As time passes, the distance between us increases, and our kicks become faster and harder. When I receive the ball, I try to slow it down as I pass it to *Tommasino*. He, however, does not follow my lead. Instead, he kicks it to *Franco* hard. In response, *Franco* kicks it to me harder still. Fearing the ball hitting one of the windows and shattering the glass, I make an attempt to stop the ball with my foot, but I fail. Instead, it hits the ground and bounces off my left knee in the direction of the ruins below us. Helplessly, I watch the ball bounce off one of the dilapidated walls and into a thorny bush.

Because I missed, I feel that I have to retrieve the ball. I run across the front of the palazzo and down the pathway that leads to the ruins. I determine the best spot to climb the wall for retrieval. Down one side, to the nearest corner, and then about three-quarters of the way up the other side. From there, and with a manageable stretch, I should be able to inch the ball close enough to grab. In the meantime, *Tommasino e Franco* have joined me amongst the rubble and are making an adventure out of it. They've taken a dangerous shortcut and slid down the steep side of the courtyard. They're now on the wall opposite me, brandishing tree branches as if they were swords like pirates on a ship. While I am awash with fear.

All I want is to retrieve the ball and go back. I don't want to play anymore. But before I reach the ball, I'm waist-deep in the bush. Panic-stricken and as if driven by some supernatural power, I grab the ball and throw it towards the open pathway. I climb up the wall, then down. No hesitation. And then I feel a searing pain in both my bare legs. I look down to see rivulets of blood rushing to my socks. Several thorns have carved their signatures into my skin.

Another wave of panic. But this time, no supernatural powers. I think of *Mamma*. What will I tell her? How will I explain? Can I hide what has happened? The scratches on my legs. The blood on my shorts. My socks. How can I? I cannot. She will find out. And she will kill me!

Being the sons of a pharmacist, *Franco e Tommasino* prove to be resourceful. They lead me to their house, where they produce antiseptic and gauzes and help me clean up. Fortunately, the scratches aren't as deep as they appear. With the disinfectant, the rivers of blood become almost invisible. We also do a good job at lightening the bloodstains from the edges of my shorts and the tops of my socks.

That evening, I succeed in hiding my calamity from *Mamma*. Finally, when I'm in the safety of my bed, I thank the Trinity for helping me, even though I had sinned gravely by disobedience, deceit, and lies. And I promise that, from that moment on, I will be a good boy. As penance, I give myself ten *Gloria al Padres*, and, in my head, I begin to recite them while keeping count. I don't know how many I manage before falling asleep.

Horror strikes me the following morning when I wake up to discover bloodstains all over my white sheets. Both, top and bottom! The rivers of blood had surged, once again! My repentance... my prayers... my promises... had not been enough. Who was I fooling? God was angry! I was a sinner! I deserved to be punished! No escape!

1960s – Summer – Boys at play down by the river

2009 – Summer – Boys at play under bridges

CHAPTER 9

L'Apprendista
The Apprentice

TODAY, ITALY CELEBRATES ITS FREEDOM FROM NAZISM. IT IS *LA Festa della Liberazione*, a holiday for me but not for *Mamma e Papà*. I'm happy because *Papà* said I can go with him to the shop. I eat all the bread in my *zuppa di latte*. Then I use both hands to lift the bowl to my lips and slurp the remaining milk. *Papà* waits to rinse the dish and put it away.

"*Loccoh. Loccoh.*" I hear *Pietro* calling from the courtyard below. I know it's *Pietro* because he's the only one who calls *Papà Loccoh. Papà's* name is *Rocco. Papà* goes to the bedroom and opens the balcony door. He throws the shop keys down to *Pietro*. "Go open up. You can start removing the stitches from *Gaetano's* trousers. They're on the bench. I want them ready for the iron. And if he happens to show up, tell *Orazio* to sweep the floor. I'll be down in a few minutes."

Zio Mario owns the tailor shop on *Via Angelo Santilli* where *Papà* works. Because his hands and feet swell, *Zio Mario* doesn't come to the shop every day; he relies on *Papà* to manage his clientele. Right now, there are three boys learning to become tailors: *Pietro, Orazio,* and *Roberto. Pietro* is the youngest. When he completed Grade 5 last year, his mother asked *Papà* if he could take him on because *Pietro* was finished with school and needed to learn a trade. *Pietro* has trouble saying the letter "r." People laugh at him because he talks funny, but I don't mind when he calls me *Bluno*.

Orazio is the oldest and has been at the shop the longest. *Papà* says that he'll never learn to be anything because he's too lazy. Some days, *Orazio* doesn't show up for work. No one knows where he hides, including his father. Not long ago, I heard one of *Papà*'s friends say that *Orazio*'s father chained him to a tree for two whole days and nights so he wouldn't run away again. In school, he skipped classes all the time. Eventually he was kicked out because he was too old. "*Orazio* is a wild one!" everybody says.

The third learner in the shop is my cousin *Roberto*. He is *Zio Mario*'s only son. *Roberto* is twelve, three years older than me. After fifth grade, he said that he didn't want to go to middle school, so *Zio Mario* makes him go to the shop instead. I don't think *Roberto* wants to become a tailor either. He's always late, even after *Papà* scolds him.

Mamma e Papà argue about not having enough money to pay the rent. *Mamma* tells *Papà* that he works for next to nothing. "You better watch out. You'll be working for your nephew some day! He'll be the boss!" she cries out. *Mamma* thinks that *Zio Mario* is using *Papà* to teach his son how to sew so that, in the future, when *Roberto* is older, he will manage the tailor shop and not *Papà*.

When *Papà* and I arrive at the shop, *Pietro* and *Orazio* are fooling around. As soon as they see *Papà*, they freeze.

"*Pietro*, are you done with the trousers?" *Papà* asks.

In reply, *Pietro* stutters a negative response, turning to *Orazio* to indicate that he was hiding them. *Papà* gives *Orazio* a stern look and, magically, the trousers appear on the table, the stitching untouched. *Papà* grabs the pants and violently throws them at *Pietro*'s face.

"Get to work!" he yells. *Pietro* barely manages to cover his eyes. Then *Papà* turns to me. "You, go sit at the machine and do your homework! Quietly." Finally, he turns to *Orazio*. "And you, good for nothing *deficiente* (moron), take the broom and sweep the floor! Before I break it over your head!"

My homework is arithmetic problems and a reading assignment. The problems I find easy to solve, but I have a hard time completing the reading because I'm constantly distracted. The chapter is about the conflict between the Romans and the Etruscans in 390 B.C. *Papà* screams at *Orazio*, and my mind wanders. When I grow up, I don't want to be a tailor. I don't want to be like *Orazio*. Still, I'd like to know where he disappears to. A passerby says, "*Buongiorno*." I look up, but no one is there. I wonder if *Roberto* is coming today.

I wish I were in school. I like school. Better still, I wish I were home playing. I must finish reading the chapter. I lose my place and start over. I should pay attention. After Grade 5, I want to go to middle school And after middle school, to high school. And maybe to university? But *Mamma* says that we have no money. "University is for rich people," she says. We are poor. I lose my place again! Back to the beginning. Maybe *La Maestra* is right to tell *Papà* that I daydream a lot. Maybe I have no choice but to be a tailor like *Papà*. Or a cobbler like *Papà's Papà*. No. I must concentrate on what I'm reading. I'm almost at the end. Good!

"*Papà*, I did all my homework. Can I go to *Antonio's* next door?" I ask.

"Yes, but don't cause any trouble. And stay close to the shop."

I open the door to the cobbler's shop and immediately am hit with a rancid mixture of rot, polish, and *pece*, the special paste cobblers use to whet the twine when hand-stitching leather to soles. '*Ndònih gliu scarpar* (*Antonio* the cobbler), isn't there. I'm glad to see *Germano*, the apprentice, there alone. He greets me with a grin.

"Eh, *Brunellino*, I was just thinking about you. Come in. Have a seat."

He leans to one side and grabs a bundle of old publications from under his chair. "Look what I've saved for you." He offers me the stack. "You can cut out as many pictures as you want, but only if you come with me on my break," he says, releasing his hold of my treasure-trove.

Without hesitation, I nod agreement and go sit on the spare stool beside him. I flip through the papers looking for cutouts.

"I want to show you something very important," he continues, "but you have to keep it a secret. Can you do that?" he asks and hands me a pair of scissors.

"Sure, I can," I answer carelessly.

Germano is much older than me, but I'm almost as tall as he is. He has straight black hair that he's always combing back over his head with his hand and comb so that it shines like the shoes he polishes. He smells like the shop, even when we're outside. As he locks the door, he reassures himself one more time. "Bru, swear to me that you will not tell anyone."

I place my right hand on my heart and say, "*Lo giuro.*" (I swear.)

Sant'Elia was heavily bombed during World War II, leaving many buildings in ruins. *Papà* grew up during that time and is always telling me about the misery of war: "The Americans, the Germans, the English, the whole world, may they all go to hell, dropped bombs on *Sant'Elia*. Like rain. It was the end of the world! I lost my mother, *buonanima* (bless her soul), to one of those damned bombs. *La Nonna* you never met. She died right in front of *Palazzo Gagliardi*, where you play soccer! *La Guerra, per Dio!* What was I, a couple of years older than you are now? Not even. Forced to leave home to hide in the mountains. Like gypsies. Running scared. Hungry. And practically naked! That's sacrifice! Not what you complain about. You, with a roof over your head. A full stomach. Warm clothes on your back. No holes in your shoes. And no patches on your pants. *Porca Madonna.* And if that wasn't enough, you're learning to read and write! *Schifosa miseria.* Me? I barely made it to Grade 5. After the war, I had to help out. I had no choice but to learn a trade. And I've been working ever since. You wanna talk about suffering? About sacrifice, huh? Your mother and I, we have lived in misery. We know all about ... *fame e sofferenza*. Not you, my son. Not you! You don't know the first thing! *Mannaggia la miseria!* (Damn misery!)"

Germano and I walk to the nearby ruins. As I follow through the rubble, I recall *Papà's* lecture. I'm careful not to step on the piles of *merda* that are everywhere. The remains of the old buildings have become a public washroom. We go to a far corner where no one can see us. Facing each other, *Germano* pulls out his wallet from the back pocket of his trousers, opens it, takes out two photographs, and shows them to me. They are of two naked women. Who are they? Is this the secret? *Germano* guides me to hold the pictures in such a way that he can see them. He looks at the photos as he unbuckles his belt and unbuttons his fly. I want to turn around but continue to hold the pictures as shown. Why is he not turning around if he has to pee? He doesn't. And he doesn't pee either. Instead, he drops his trousers and underwear to his ankles. Shocked, I stare at the dark hairy clump between his legs and feel heat rising to my face. Unconcerned with my feelings, *Germano* rubs and shakes loose the cluster. Stunned by how large everything is, I stare at the hair between his legs. Why is it not greasy and straight like the hair on his head?

"Here, give me your hand. Touch it. I'll show you how to make this *cazzo* really hard. Let's do it together," he says.

I pull back in disgust. And fear the presence of *Mamma*. She doesn't like it when I say a *parolaccia*. "Bad words make bad people!" She tells me all the time. *Cazzo*, I know, is a very bad word. And dirty too. I'm ashamed even when *Germano* says it. I feel my face burning up.

"I don't want to," I mutter. What I want is to run away from here. But I can't move. And I can't speak! Words don't come. I stare, frozen, thinking, it's so big.

Germano wraps his hand around it. He squeezes, and it grows bigger. He pulls back the skin, and a pink, shiny bulb emerges. There's a hole at the top that looks like a tiny mouth gasping for air. My arms have fallen by my sides, and my hand is still hanging on to the photos. *Germano* grunts as he reaches over to snatch the pictures from me, his eyes searching the naked women. His right hand moves up and down. The pink head appears and disappears, like a blinking light. Again he tells me, *"Acchiappa' quà, Bru. Accuscì."* Grab it here, Bruno. Like this. Again, I refuse. He stops for a moment and then grabs my hand forcefully and guides it around the shaft. I try to pull away, but his hold is too strong.

"Hey, that's part of our deal, remember?" he says.

I try to remember that part of the deal. My hand disappears under his. Together both hands slide up and down. Even with it squished, I can sense the difference in texture between the palm and the back of my hand: on one side, I feel softness, and on the other, roughness.

"Squeeze hard, *Bru*. Like this. Go faster."

My mouth fills with saliva. My throat is dry. I'd like to swallow but can't. I want to spit it out, but I can't do that either. I don't want to open my mouth and let dirt in. I don't want to breathe. I taste the air. I don't want to see, but my eyes are stuck open! There's ringing in my ears and in my head. The noise is getting louder. Everything stop, please! I want to go home. *Mamma. Papà.* Don't be angry with me. I'm not a bad boy! It's not my fault!

Suddenly, the grip on my hand releases. I remain frozen in place. *Germano* spits in the palm of his hand and rubs the spit on the shiny head. His hand then returns to grasp mine. The motion starts up again. The grip tight once more. The difference now is that I feel the spit on the back of my hand. My stomach heaves. I have to wash my hand! Let me go! I'm going to be sick! The screams echo inside my head. My lips are sealed.

Reluctantly, I swallow to catch a breath. *Germano* is in another world altogether. He doesn't care about me. I'm not his friend anymore! He holds me too tight. He controls my arm. It goes up and down, all by itself. Very fast.

Germano moans and the up-and-down motion stops. But the grip on my hand gets tighter. Both hands push down. The skin is stretched tight. *Germano* groans, and a white, creamy liquid spurts out of the tiny mouth. The hands, one inside the other, squeeze even tighter. More liquid squirts out. I worry that it's going to hit me. My skin. Not on my clothes! I want to move out of the way. And then the grip is gone. And so is the hardness. My hand is finally free, but I don't know where to put it. It's dirty. I raise it mid-air and hold it there. *Germano* gasps. Is he okay? I see him peripherally. He pulls up his underwear and then his pants. Buttons up his fly, tucks in his shirt, and buckles his belt. With both hands, he brushes his greasy hair back over his head and says, "Get a move on, Bru. I have to go back to work."

We walk back. *Germano* whistles "*O Sole Mio.*" His stride is fast. I run to keep up. I don't mind because I flap my arms in the air and let the wind clean my hands. The door to the shop is open. '*Ndònih gliu scarpar* (*Antonio* the cobbler) is sitting at his chair. Quickly, *Germano* goes to his workstation. As he settles in, he winks at me to say, "Eh, don't forget our deal!"

I remember the cuttings and, forgetting my dirty hands, reach deep in my pockets to reassure myself that the wads of pictures are still there.

"I won't forget," I nod back.

Papà is busy with a customer. I sneak past him and go to the table at the back of the shop. It's not in use, so I can play. I decide to re-enact the decisive battle between *Roma e L'Etruria*. I use a new box of shiny buttons to recruit my Roman army, and old buttons of various shapes and sizes to represent the enemy. Once and for all, today I will settle the score between the Romans and those slimy Etruscans...

From my high vantage point, I examine my legions. Row upon row of shiny shields and shimmering swords. Uniform, orderly and ready to fight for me. I'm as proud of my troops as they are of me. Across the field, I snicker at the enemy. Hopelessly disorganized. A mass of humanity awaiting their onslaught. I ride tall on my horse, feeling strong and invincible. The red plumage of my helmet bounces up and down with the trotting of the mare... I see my arm moving up-and-down... I see *Germano* in control... Stop that! No distractions! The men wait for my command... I tighten my grip around... *il cazzo di Germano*... No!... it's around the sword! My sword!... Again... the soldiers wait for the signal... my right hand holds the sword... tightly... as I raise it and... a white liquid... No! No interference!... I raise my sword high over my head and yell out... Attack!... Attack!... Attack!

1960s – Bruno

1961 – Bruno's Grade 5 graduation

CHAPTER 10

Don Bruno
Father Bruno

YOUNG AND ENERGETIC, *DON MARIO* CAME TO FILL THE VACANCY left behind by old and tired *Don Benedetto*. The latter, of a family deeply rooted in our community, was born, raised, and, not long ago, buried in *Sant'Elia Fiumerapido*. The former, a stranger to us, was sent to revitalize our people by the bishop of the Abbey of Montecassino. *La Chiesa Madre* was the church from where our new priest would lead his flock. And, across from it, *Palazzo Gagliardi* was where he would reside.

Before *Don Mario* could take up residence, the building was to undergo a major renovation. The second floor was gutted and the three separate apartments converted into one integral living space. The creation of this new suite had advantages and disadvantages for the tenants that remained. On the positive side was the introduction of running water. This meant toilets added to the rudimentary lavatories and washbasins installed in the basic kitchens. Another benefit was the much-needed rewiring and upgraded lighting of the stairwell. There was a negative side, however. Although the structure was owned by the abbey, the renovation project was not charity. The changes came with a significant increase in the monthly rent, which was not welcome news for *Mamma e Papà*.

Prior to *Don Mario*'s arrival, the town's rumor mill was very lively. Although nobody had actually met or seen the priest, everyone seemed to have formed an opinion about him. Some were laced with warnings. Others with expectations. When he finally arrived and became known to more people, the liveliness of the gossip did not subside; instead, it expanded exponentially. In the shops, in the streets, in the portals of buildings, townsfolk whispered a web of intrigue about the new priest.

Don Mario? He is not so young after all... but he is good looking... He will be good for our community... Oh, but he's sly, that's for sure... I don't trust him... If you can't trust your priest, who can you trust? He's got so much energy... And smarts... He seems to have an eye for young women... But he's a priest... He's so sophisticated... A go-getter... Very social... He's good for our youth... He is visionary... Lock up your daughters, my friends... He's a northerner... No, he's not... He's got our boys off the streets... And that's good... He's bad news for our girls... Is it? You know, you can't trust northerners... He has family in *Milano*... No, *Venezia*... He's a crafty one... He speaks so well... He's on a recruit mission... The bishop sent him here for a reason, I tell you... Those sermons on Sundays... Boys and girls, watch out!... He was looking right at me... He's quick-witted... A matchmaker... He has a nephew... He is cunning... A nephew?... He's looking for a wife?... *Don Mario?*... No, his nephew... Ohh... Hmm... Ahh... Ehh...

The community of *Sant'Elia Fiumerapido* comprises seven thousand residents, give or take. It boasts two separate dioceses, each with its respective priest and church. I don't know if or when the two factions ever competed with one another, but with the arrival of the new priest, the invisible boundary soon became evident. Our side was led by the forward-thinking *Don Mario*. Their side was led by the stale conservative *Don Michele*. Our church was *La Chiesa Madre*, situated at the heart of the town. Their church was located at the back of the municipal gardens.

Like a shepherd and his sheep, the wealth of each jurisdiction could be measured by the number of old women in attendance at their daily mass, and by the number of young people they were able to add to their flock. Generally, men didn't figure in the comparison, for they preferred a game of cards to sitting in a pew beside their wife and children. Both churches had an equal number of devoted old women; however, when it came to the younger generations, *Don Mario* was the winner by a long shot.

One of the first things *Don Mario* implemented when he arrived in *Sant'Elia* was to organize the youth. For us boys, he created a social ambiance where, instead of running in and out of the town's ruins and playing mischievous games, we could congregate in a rented space near the church to read books and magazines, play board games, ping-pong, and foosball. Or, if we preferred the outdoors, play soccer or volleyball in the courtyard. He balanced this social element with an equal dose of responsibility. We were all trained to become "qualified" altar boys. It became a sort of competition. We learned the Latin liturgy. We practiced the various moves and positions during celebratory services. And we competed for the leading roles. The boy who was picked to lead the team of six at the altar did so with honor and pride.

For the girls and young women, *Don Mario* solicited their involvement in sprucing up the interior of the church. Soon, the altars of *La Chiesa Madre* began to sparkle like never before, each adorned with bouquets of fresh flowers beautifully arranged. Brass candelabras freed of dripping wax and shined to a gleam.

Floors swept and washed to a new luster. The sacristy, where *Don Mario*'s liturgical garments were kept, was organized and maintained to a new level of fastidiousness.

Perhaps it was because I lived in the same building as he did. Or because I was very shy. Or because I was seen to be more malleable. *Don Mario* picked me when I was seven or eight to join the boys' club. For a long while, I was the youngest and the shortest, and, therefore, easily bullied by the other boys. They gave me the name *Mezzo Metro*, Half-Meter. Don Mario must have sensed the disparity because he began to keep an eye on me. He kept me close to him. As a valet, almost. He often invited me to his apartment. He gave me books to read. He sent me on small errands to the store for some grocery item, a pack of cigarettes, or a newspaper. He asked me to be there, in his suite, while one of the single young women was cleaning or cooking for him. And he always rewarded me. A cookie. An illustrated book. A soda. A snack. A Latin-to-Italian dictionary. A choco-late. I was privileged. I felt special.

Being *Mezzo Metro* had its benefits. Sometimes. I was able to almost disappear into a corner when surrounded by adults having uncensored conversations. This was especially true when I was in *Papà*'s shop. Late in the evenings, his buddies would come in to chat and brag with him and spread the latest scandals. As they warmed up in discussion, I silently melted into the background and kept my ears fully open. *Don Mario* often dominated the slander. And with him, young and older women alike were thrown into the fire. They talked of daughters, sisters, and mothers I had come to know, of course. I listened attentively and continued to fit one piece after another into the puzzle I held in my mind.

The nuns that ran the local kindergarten school were not spared from the end-of-day smear. I remember an evening not long ago, when *Zio Ettore* dropped in at the shop to shoot the breeze with *Papà*. *Zio Ettore* considered himself quite the womanizer for he was young, unattached, and unencumbered. So, to make *Papà* jealous, he often stopped at the shop to boast about one of his latest adventures. As they chatted, something that *Zio Ettore* said caught my attention: "I wanna do me a nun some day!" The phrase shocked me at first, but then its seed began to germinate and spread in my brain like a disease. "Do me a nun," what did he mean by that? Marry a nun, or rape a nun? Can he do that? How? I suppose if she left the order, she and *Zio Ettore* could marry one another. And I would have an ex-nun for an aunt. But what if he wanted to rape one? Would that not be an unpardonable sin? Of the worst kind? The question of how became my disease. It persisted in my head for a long time, especially when I saw one of the sisters in church or when one of the younger ones was with *Don Mario*. Did *Don Mario* want to do himself a nun, too?

With the arrival of *Don Mario*, *Sant'Elia Fiumerapido* experienced a resurgence of sorts. It felt livelier somehow. Definitely more vigorous. The war seemed a distant memory. Life had promise... or this is how I saw it when I was in Grade 5.

By the time I was ten, I had successfully completed elementary school and thus surpassed *Mamma e Papà* in their respective educations. In October 1962, I was enrolled in the first of three years of *Le Scuole Medie*, middle school. I was learning Italian, Latin, and French, as well as physics and algebra and other subjects, each taught by a different *professore*. By this time, I had already received my first communion and confirmation. And if that wasn't enough, I was an accomplished and well-liked altar boy.

Everyone in the diocese knew me as *Don Mario's* favorite. And I was proud of it. When selected to do so, I climbed the bell tower to wake the town to the first mass of the day at 6:00 A.M. And in my always-spotless *chirichetto* uniform, I single-handedly served mass. On some festive occasions, while other boys concocted excuses to escape the altar, I served up to four masses in a single day. In the eyes of some worshipers, I was becoming a little saint.

It was around this time that the future of my education became a frequent topic of discussion between *Mamma e Papà*. Usually it was at the kitchen table within my earshot. Their conclusion was always the same: with a Grade 8 education, I would have accomplished a hell of a lot more than either one of them. Sometimes they got into heated arguments, especially if one of them had crossed paths with *La Maestra* or *Don Mario*. Then they would pepper the conversation by cursing one or the other, or both together, for not minding their own business.

La Maestra seals my five years of elementary school education by saying, "*Bruno è capace.*" I have potential.

La Professoressa welcomes me into middle school. At the end of my first year, *la Prima Media*, she conveys to *Mamma e Papà* that, "*Sarebbe un peccato se Bruno non potesse continuare a studiare, almeno fino al liceo.*" (It would be a sin if Bruno can't continue my studies, as a minimum, through to high school.)

Lina, the cobbler's wife, says to Mamma half-jokingly when they meet on the street, "*Sé Bruno s vo spusà la Rita mè, tera prima studià p rvntà mierg o avvocàt pché la Rita mè è nu gioièl!*" If I want to marry her daughter, Rita, I must study to become a doctor or a lawyer, because *her Rita* is a treasure!

And at every opportunity, *Don Mario* reminds both *Mamma e Papà* that he has the one and only solution for me: *"Non dimenticate, io ho l'unica soluzione per Bruno! Pensateci bene!"* They must think it over carefully!

Don Mario is well aware of my parents' financial situation. He knows they are struggling to put food on the table and keep a roof over their heads. He describes a scenario that allows me to reach whatever level of higher education I aspire to and that won't cost *Mamma e Papà* a penny! *Don Mario* also explains that if at any point during my studies I don't want to pursue priesthood, I can simply walk away. As he finally put it, there is absolutely nothing to lose, but everything to gain. All they have to do is give him the green light.

When they're not yelling at each other, *Mamma e Papà* make fun of me at the kitchen table and call me *Don Bruno*. They say they can see me donning the long black cassock, a sparkling white clerical collar around my neck and leather sandals like the monks wear on my feet, going door-to-door asking for donations. Then they diverge and, in mockery, ask each other what it is that priests wear under their long cassocks. Underpants, or nothing at all? As their vulgarity continues, so does the heat of shame on my cheeks. I am so embarrassed that I hide in the other room but continue to listen to their ridicule.

As I see it, after I complete *la Terza Media* I have but two choices: join the seminary to become a priest or join *Papà* to become a tailor. Neither choice is mine, however. *Mamma e Papà* hold total authority.

No. I do not want to be a priest. No. I do not want to be a tailor. No. I do not want to disappoint *Don Mario*. No. I do not want to add to *Mamma's* woes. No. I do not want to make *Papà* any angrier. No. I do not want *la Professoressa* to be disheartened about my ability. No. I do not know how to express the thoughts that roam in my head. And yes. I will do as you say.

A day doesn't go by that *Mamma e Papà* don't argue about their precarious finances. They always end up at the same conclusion: they have no one to help them. And that they have no means to access the greedy bureaucracy.

"If you want to get ahead in this godforsaken town, you have to knock on *their* door with your foot!" *Mamma* would cry out. "But I have no chicken to pluck for *La Signora!*" she would add. And *Papà* would continue with, "And I haven't got a bottle of wine to give to them. *Signori del cazzo!*" Then *Mamma*, "Or a cup of flour to bake a loaf of bread." And then *Papà*, "Not even a stolen piece of cloth to make a pair of fuckin' shorts for their precious little *Signorini! Per Dio!* What did the war accomplish? I ask you. It made the rich richer and the less fortunate hungrier!"

At first, I didn't know what it meant to knock on someone's door with a foot, but I soon figured it out. If a person uses the foot, it means that the hands are occupied, or that they're carrying something. A chicken, a cake, perhaps? *Mamma e Papà* both agreed that we were stuck. We had come from poverty, and we remained in poverty. And I was too. And so were a lot of other people.

The poor were not the landowners, the lawyers, the doctors, or the teachers. And they were not the peasants in the mountains with a little patch of dirt to grow enough food to feed their families and then some. They were the tradesmen who couldn't secure a regular income. The men returning from military service who couldn't find gainful employment. And the young families that couldn't provide shelter for their children. They were desperate people who, given no other choice, traded their misery for an ounce of courage. Brave enough to venture into places unknown in search of a different future.

Papà, unfortunately perhaps, had been too eager to start a family to just pick up and go. Or perhaps he had no choice but to marry. With a wife and two kids in tow, it was much more difficult to emigrate. But *Papà* never lost his enthusiasm or his determination. He applied and kept on applying to every nation, near and afar, looking for hard-working men and women. Finally, after many years, his efforts were rewarded. In the summer of 1964, when I had successfully completed *la Seconda Media*, he boarded *La Vulcania* to go to Canada. A new door was opening, one that promised myriad possibilities. And opportunities.

I close my eyes. I imagine the new world... I am on a boat... with *Cristoforo Colombo*... the *Santa Maria*... approaching shore... thick forests beyond... hiding behind massive tree trunks, curious natives intrigued by the newcomers... I get out of the boat... sword in hand... except I hold it from the opposite end... but it's not a sword... it's a crucifix... my uniform is not of a centurion but of a monk... I am a missionary... I am a priest... I have come to save the heathen... I am *Padre Bruno*... sent on a mission by... the Bishop of Montecassino... no, I never met the bishop... *Don Mario*... yes, *Don Mario* sends me... I am to build a new church... it will be called *La Chiesa Madre*... the whole population is congregating... they have come to hear me preach... they search for knowledge... they need guidance... *Padre Bruno* has so much to teach them... one voice says, "Speak to us, *Padre*"... then another, and another... "speak... speak... speak to us, *Padre!*"

With a jolt, I wake up from the dream screaming, "No. No, I am not *Padre Bruno*. I am here for the same reason as you are. To learn!"

La Chiesa Madre (Mother Church) - interior

1960s – Bruno, the altar boy, in procession with *Don Mario*

2011 - *La Chiesa Madre* (Mother Church) - exterior

CHAPTER 11

La Partenza
The Departure

FRIDAY, THE FOURTH OF DECEMBER, 1964. EXACTLY ONE WEEK before my thirteenth birthday. As the train slows down, the hiss and screech of brakes announce the final stop. The journey from Italy to Canada is at an end. And so is my battle with the invincible ocean. For nine whole days and ten long nights, I fought in vain. I threw up when there was nothing left to throw up. I recoiled at the bitter taste of bile. I begged for clemency. Drained, I stepped onto solid ground and was led onto a train. Another two days and two nights. A respite. The monotonous clickety-clack washed away my nausea and deadened my hunger. It was cloudy when we left the Port of Naples. It was cloudy when we reached Pier 21. And it's cloudy when we step out on the sidewalk outside Union Station. And cold.

Sunday, the twenty-second of November, 1964. *Mamma*, *Fulvia*, and I are on board the big ship, the MS *Vulcania*. From the side rail, we look down at the small group that came to see us off: *Nonna*; *Zia Nina*, *Mamma's* older sister; and *Zio Ettore*, *Mamma's* younger brother. And *Americo*, the taxi driver. The two women stand side-by-side in the middle of the platform.

Handkerchiefs in hand, they look in our direction, turn to console one another, and dab their eyes. *Zio Ettore* stands discretely away from them. Hands in his pockets, he peruses the surroundings, as if on a prowl. Away from the clusters of relations, *Americo* leans against the far wall and smokes a cigarette. We are too far apart to talk. Instead, we silently gaze in each other's direction from behind teary eyes.

I feel numb. The euphoria of the morning has dissipated. In its place is the reality of our departure. I see *Nonna*. Not there on the platform, but back in her kitchen. She summons her chickens from the window. She prepares a sandwich. She laughs so hard it makes her belly bounce up and down. She lifts her hand to her mouth to hide her lone tooth. Her beady eyes shine like diamonds.

Mamma wakes me up at 5:30 A.M. It's dark outside. Because I washed before going to bed, all I have to do this morning is get dressed. I'm excited because I will wear all new clothing. *Mamma* laid it out on her bed. I take off my pajamas. A cold shiver passes through my body. Quickly, I put on my new underwear and the woolen undershirt that *Nonna* knitted for me. The underwear is from a pack of three that *Mamma* bought at the market last Sunday. The other two pieces are packed away in the suitcase. The undershirt is itchy because I haven't worn it before. I try not to scratch because it will make it worse if I do. Next, I pull on a pair of new grey socks. They too are itchy. These socks are thicker than my usual, and they make my feet look fat. I have a second pair in the suitcase. Another shiver. Hastily, I slip into the new grey flannel trousers *Papà* made for me before he left. They are soft and a little too big. *Papà* said that I will grow into them. Next, I put on my white shirt. This is the same shirt I wore for my First Communion a year ago. *Mamma* made me try it on yesterday to see if it still fit. I tuck the front and back tails inside my pants and button the fly. The last piece on the bed is a blue wool sweater. *Mamma* bought it a couple of days ago at *Zia*

Lina's shop. *Zia Lina* said that she was giving her a very good price, almost the same as what she had paid for it! After we got home, *Mamma* said *Zia Lina* is a liar. The cement floor is cold. I look for my black boots. *Antonio* the cobbler made them especially for the Canadian snow. Even though I have thick socks, the boots feel loose.

"Room to grow." I hear voices in my head.

The last item to put on is my overcoat. *Papà* made this for me too just before he went to Canada. It's a big person's coat with a high collar I can unfold to keep my neck warm. And it's long. It reaches below my knees. All dressed-up, I prance around the kitchen table. For a moment, I think of *Nonna*'s white rooster. How he struts in the yard, proud and fearless. I too, right at this moment, feel proud and fearless. I am ready to face the Canadian cold.

"Bruno! Fold your pajamas and give them to me, now!" *Mamma* screams.

Americo, our driver, waits downstairs. He will drive us to *Napoli*. This is the second time I will go to *Napoli*. The first time was when *Papà* left. In August, there were more people and more cars. I remember my cousin *Roberto* was there with his father, *Zio Mario*, and his mother, *Zia Lina*. But they aren't coming today. Today, there are only two cars: *Americo*'s Mercedes and *Zio Ettore*'s *Cinquecento*. The three of us with all the suitcases and bags will be in the Mercedes, and *Nonna* and *Zia Nina* will be in the *Cinquecento*.

Americo has already made two trips up and down the stairs to our apartment. Each time he took a large suitcase down to the car. *Mamma* said that we were running late. He said that we had lots of time and told her not to worry. *Mamma* is sad. Scared. I wish she was happy. Instead, she looks like she is about to cry. *Marisa*, our next-door neighbor, has come to help her, but *Mamma* ignores her. She stands in her way. And so do I.

"Bruno, go downstairs and wait by *Americo*!" she snaps angrily.

Several of *Mamma*'s friends are gathered in the courtyard. They have come to say goodbye. When they see me, they call my name. I feel shy in my new clothes and want to turn around and go back upstairs, but *Mamma* wouldn't like that. So, my gaze to the ground, I make my way to *Americo*'s car.

"*Bruno, come sei bello.*" (Look how beautiful you are, Bruno.)

"*Adesso té né vai, eh... vai da Papà.*" (Going away now, eh... to your *Papà.*)

"*Devi essere contento, sì?*" (You must be happy, yes?)

"*Beato chi può andarsene da questo maledetto paese!*" (Blessed are those that can leave this cursed town!)

"*Eh, Lamerica!*"

Everyone compliments me for my good looks. They say that I'm a very lucky boy to be going away. Away from this wretched place. They wish they could trade places. Hide in our suitcases!

Not everybody has come down to the courtyard. Some neighbors watch from their balconies and windows. They yell down their good wishes. Some converse with others on the ground. It's hard to see their faces because it's dark. I don't see any of my friends. They must be sleeping. I am anxious. I want to be in the car and go. It feels strange to be going so far away. Away from everything. And everybody. What will Canada be like? Will I make new friends? Will I like my new school? Will the teachers like me? Will my friends here miss me? Will I ever see them again? *Felicetto. Tommasino. Franco. Nino. Paoletto. Roberto.*

"*Buon viaggio, Lenù!*" (Safe trip, *Lenù!*) someone blurts out from one of the balconies. And, as if on cue, everybody turns their attention towards the *portone* of *Palazzo Gagliardi. Mamma* has finally descended. Like sheep, the crowd in the *piazzetta* moves towards her as she slowly makes her way to the car. It feels like a market day with all the cries and hollers. Everyone has something to relay to *Mamma.* A hug. A kiss. A wish for a safe journey. A request for a postcard from Canada. A letter every now and then. A report on how the family is managing. A reminder to not be forgotten. A message to pass on to a brother or a cousin that lives in Canada.

Americo shifts the gear and the vehicle starts to crawl forward. Outside, an overcast sky with the threat of rain. Finally, some quietude. The only sound is that of the rolling tires driving on the cobblestones of *Via Angelo Santilli*. Because I suffer from motion sickness, I sit in the front with *Americo*. *Mamma* and *Fulvia* sit in the back. It helps if I face forward and have access to fresh air. Hopefully, I won't throw up this time. *Americo* faces forward. I am on my knees, turned around. *Mamma* is twisted to look outside the rear window. Her friends, bunched together in the middle of the street, wave. As the car speeds up, the cluster becomes smaller. When the car turns the corner, it disappears. *Mamma* turns to face forward. Tears stream down her face. I too turn around and cry.

1960s - *Papà* leaves his friends and his native town for foreign lands

August 1964 – *Papà* goes to Canada – Port of Naples Pier

Lower photo is a detail of photo above – from left-to-right:
Nonna, Zio Ettore, Zio Mario, L'Avvocato e La Signora Lucia (the lawyer and his wife, *Zia Nina*'s employer), *Zia Lina, Zia Nina, Fulvia, Mamma* (crying), *Bruno e Americo* (seated near the wall)

CHAPTER 12
La Vulcania
The MS Vulcania

We are leaving port. The ship horn is loud. One blast, then another. The vibration resonates in my body. My hypnotic trance is broken. Chaos. Passengers rush about. They furrow their way towards the stern. Some extend themselves over the railing and wave to people below. On the platform, friends move in the opposite direction to catch a last glimpse of a loved one. Unknown names fill the air. The wind disperses the cries. The rumble of engines propels us further apart. The once familiar landscape retreats to the horizon. Exiled, the liner becomes a holding cell, the ocean the jailer.

"Let's go find our cabin," *Mamma* says.

Our third-class cabin is in steerage, the least desirable part of the ship. And the cheapest fare available. This was the most *Papà* could afford. We share the space with *commara Marcella* and her seven-week-old baby, *Sabina*. *Marcella* is seventeen years old. Like *Mamma*, she is going to Canada where she will join her husband. They were married in January and had the baby in September. We were at their wedding. *Mamma e Papà* are *Sabina's* godparents.

Mamma is the oldest. She leads the way, even though she doesn't know exactly where our cabin is. She pulls my younger sister, *Fulvia*, by the hand as she figures a path. *Marcella* holds her baby close to her chest and tries to keep up with *Mamma*. I, in turn, follow *Marcella*. Every so often, *Mamma* turns around to make sure we're all following.

We first walk towards the center of the ship and go down a wide flight of stairs. We then go to the right and follow a long corridor to a much narrower and longer set of stairs. When we reach the bottom, we turn sharply to the right, but it's a wrong turn. We go back and turn to the left instead and go along a passageway until we reach the same number as on the key. *Mamma* inserts the key in the lock and turns it clockwise to open the door. Our baggage has been delivered, and it covers the whole floor. *Mamma* tells us all to wait outside while she does some organizing inside. *Sabina* starts to cry. *Marcella* says she is hungry. I retrace earlier steps to get away from the howling. Back in the passageway, I hear the rumble of motors. I place my hand on the metal wall and feel the vibrations of the engines. In the air, I smell a sickly mix of diesel fuel and kitchen exhaust. The kitchen must be nearby. The offensive combination hangs in the air like an invisible cloud. I wish for a breath of fresh sea air, but there is none to be had.

The cabin comprises two bunk beds on either side of the door, and a mirror vanity over a little porcelain sink on the wall directly across. *Mamma* has slid the suitcases under each of the bottom beds and divided the sacks at the foot of each of the four beds. She has also decided where we sleep. *Fulvia* and I are assigned the two top bunks. I climb up the ladder and sit on the edge of my bed. From there, I have a full view of *Marcella* as she prepares to quieten her baby by baring her breast to feed her. I try not to stare.

In his letters to *Mamma*, *Papà* writes that *La Vulcania* feels like it never moves. That the sea is like a plate of glass. And that he is sure I will have no problem with seasickness. But already I feel nausea coming on and the desire to lie down and go to sleep. One reason is the stench that hangs in the air, which is made worse when *Marcella* changes *Sabina's* diaper. Another reason is that I feel the slow rocking movement of the ship. With no windows, I can't tell which way we're going.

"You need to eat something," *Mamma* says. I cringe at the thought of having to open my mouth to chew, but *Mamma* insists. We follow her in search of the dining hall. The walk does little to settle my stomach; it only makes it worse. My legs are rubber. I hold on to the wall for balance. We head in the direction of loud chatter and finally arrive at a large room. It's very crowded and noisy. There are several round tables with a dozen chairs each. Most of them are occupied. We look for our assigned booth on the perimeter. I rush to sit down in order to stop my dizziness.

"Try eating some bread," *Mamma* says. I chew a piece of crust repeatedly. It's all mush, but I'm unable to swallow. All I want is to lie down and go to sleep. But *Mamma* gets angry because I'm not eating. I want her to be happy, so I swallow and take another bite from the roll. And chew and swallow again. And I feel a bit better. Before we leave, *Mamma* empties the basket of bread onto a serviette and puts it in her handbag. On our way back to our cabin, I throw up all the bread I ate in a corner. We don't clean it up. Ashamed, *Mamma* tells me to move on.

Marcella changes her baby's diaper once again. Another wave of offensive smell invades the space we share. I pull up my blanket to shield my nose. Sweat covers my body. *Mamma* washes a cloth in the sink. *Sabina* whimpers. I regurgitate. Nothing comes up except the bitter bile. The air is stale. *Mamma* places a cold compress on my forehead. It feels nice. The enemy continues to advance. The fetid diaper. The rancid fumes from the kitchen. The pungent odor from diesel fuel. The sour taste of saliva. The musty feel of sweat. In delirium, I surrender.

Of the ten days at sea, I spend most of my time in the cabin, lying on my bed. A couple of times I attempt to visit the dining hall, but it always turns out the same. The ship is relentless in its rocking and rolling. *Mamma, Marcella,* and *Fulvia* have begun to suffer seasickness. But not as bad as me. They are able to go up on deck and to the dining room. The only food I can tolerate is the small bread rolls with a thick crust. *Mamma* has befriended a *cameriere* (waiter) who provides her with a daily supply of these rolls. All other foods make me regurgitate. I remember a movie I saw not long ago in *Sant'Elia* called *Pane e Vino*. It was the story of a poor family that didn't have much food except for bread and wine. In contrast, I live on *pane e acqua*, bread and water. I remember it was funny, but it doesn't make me laugh now. I bury my nose in my pillow to stop the stench.

The sun is shining today. I venture a walk to the outside deck. It's cold and windy, and the ocean is wavy with white caps. It is not the sheet of glass *Papà* described in his letter to *Mamma*. But the air is fresh. I take a deep breath and taste the salt air on my tongue. I follow the waves down to where they hit the side of the ship. In tandem, I heave and roll with the swell below. I hold on to the rail as I turn my stomach inside out. The waves just keep on coming. My head feels heavy. It pulls the rest of my body forward while an unexpected force pulls me back. A fellow passenger,

"You shouldn't hang your head over the railing that way. It's liable to pull you over and you could fall."

I am embarrassed. Then scared. I go back to the cabin and say nothing of what happened. I promise myself to remain in the cabin the rest of the journey. I hang on to the memory of the fresh air.

November 1964 – On the MS *Vulcania* … to rejoin *Papà*
From center to right: *Bruno, Fulvia, Marcella* with *Sabina* and *Mamma*

November 1964 – Dining on the big ship
From left-to-right: *Marcella* with *Sabina, Mamma, Fulvia* and *Bruno*

CHAPTER 13
L'Arrivo
The Arrival

I KNOW WHY *CRISTOFORO COLUMBO* KISSED THE GROUND WHEN
he got off the *Santa Maria* in 1492. He was seasick. Just like me!

It is Wednesday morning, the second of December, 1964. The
ship has finally stopped moving. We are docked at Pier 21, Port
of Halifax, Nova Scotia. Although it's been just over a week
since we left *il Porto di Napoli*, it feels much longer than that. I
remember comparing the map of Italy to one of North America.
Without considering the different scales, I located the four
points of interest and determined that Toronto is about the same
distance from Halifax as *Sant'Elia* is from *Napoli*. Therefore, I
concluded, *Papà* is not far.

Like tributaries, ship passengers disgorge from corridors into
a cavernous hall inside a massive building. In a beeline, my sister,
Marcella, and I follow *Mamma*. *Mamma* carries two large bags in
one hand and, with the other, pulls *Fulvia* behind her. *Marcella*
stays close to my sister, keeping an eye on *Mamma*. With both
arms, she holds *Sabina* to her chest. I run after *Marcella*. I carry

two heavy bags, one in each hand. I don't know why *Mamma* is in a hurry. Are we going to miss the train?

Row upon row of wooden benches fill the hall. Soon, every row overflows with people from the ship and their belongings. It's very noisy, but as each group marks its territory, the room becomes quieter, except for the stifled cry of a baby here and there. The fluorescent lights in the high ceiling make everyone's face look pale and sickly. *Mamma* looks worried, with dark bags under her roving eyes. Nervous tears held back, I wish I could do something to help her. Every so often, a voice blurts something out of speakers mounted on the wall. We wait for our name to be called.

"*E-li-na… Pa-na-ssi-o-ni… E-li-na… Pa-na-ssi-o-ni… Pana-ssioni… E-li-na.*"

Suddenly, *Mamma* stands up and urges us to follow her. We pick up what we had been carrying and resume the earlier queue. A man in uniform stops us at the end of the aisle and asks *Mamma* for the documents. Behind the man are rows of desks and tables. At each desk sits other uniformed men, and behind the table stands a woman or a nun. The officer looks up at *Fulvia* then at me. He turns to *Marcella* and asks for her papers. He points at us and says, "One, two, and three, yes. You, no." I recognize the extent of my English vocabulary—one, two, three, yes, no—and surmise that we are two separate families. *Marcella* must go back and wait.

The three of us are directed to one of the desks. The man checks our papers and asks *Mamma* something that she doesn't understand. He continues to talk, and *Mamma* becomes more flustered. "*I n'nt capisc. Ché vuo ra méh poveracciah?*" (I don't understand you. What do you want from poor me?) she mumbles to herself. She doesn't understand. The man shakes his head and sighs, then opens the passport and stamps one of the pages vigorously. He repeats the procedure on another strip of paper, hands everything back to *Mamma*, and points us in the direction of one of the tables. There a woman welcomes us with a big smile and gives *Mamma* a full paper bag. *Mamma* easily adds it to the other bags she is carrying. The woman then points us to yet another table, where a nun waits. She too welcomes us with a smile and gives *Fulvia* and me a small gift bag each. We end up in a waiting area with benches, chairs, and tables. I eagerly rip open my gift bag and am shocked to find a pouch of shiny glass marbles. *Palline?* I sneer to myself. I stopped playing with marbles a long time ago. I want to run back to the nun to tell her, but *Mamma* tells me to stay where I am. Instead, she offers me a perfect slice of squishy white bread from one of the two loaves she found in her "Welcome to Canada" bag.

Not long after I was born, *Papà* began to look for work outside of Italy. He had no real preference, just a deep desire to leave. He applied wherever possible: to nations close to home, such as Germany, Switzerland, and France, and to countries as far as Australia. He received two positive replies: the first in 1957 from France, the second in 1964 from Canada. France offered him a contract as a bricklayer, which he accepted without hesitation, and soon he was building walls instead of sewing trousers. Two weeks after his departure, he received a telegram from *Mamma*: "*Torna subito. Tuo figlio, molto male.*" (Come back now. Your son, very ill.) A family emergency. It was all he needed to break his contract and return home. Once back, he swore to never return to rat-infested France. Canada's offer was different. In the early 1960s Canada opened its doors to European tradespeople, which included tailors. *Papà* applied and was accepted. He left in August 1964, and within three months he had saved enough money for three one-way economy fares from *Napoli* to Toronto for the rest of his family.

On the train to Toronto, I don't get sick. Mostly, I stare out the window. All I see is snow everywhere. I could never have imagined so much empty space. There are no mountains, just frozen lakes and pine-tree forests. I recall learning about Hannibal and his crossing of the Italian Alps. His large army with its elephants. His soldiers dying in the snow. I see tree branches sticking out of the snow. They become the soldiers. Elephants sliding down steep mountain cliffs. Buried under mounds of snow. Tired and cold, one after another, they fall down and disappear. I too am a soldier. But I will not fall, because I am Hannibal. I will persevere. The sky above is a clear crisp blue.

I was wrong to assume that *Papà* was close. After two days of clickety-clack, the train finally enters Union Station and comes to a complete stop. *Papà* waits for us somewhere on the platform. I look out the window and see him, but he doesn't see me. He is looking for *Mamma*, I'm sure. He's with *Zio Vincenzo*, *Mamma's* younger brother, and *Marcella's* husband. They move towards us. I observe them; they look different than what I imagined. Strange. They look small in the crowd. We are all on the platform. A kiss on the cheek marks our reconnection. Questions and answers are exchanged about our trip and welfare. It is cold.

The trip to our new home is complicated. We follow *Zio Vincenzo* out of the station and down some stairs. We're supposedly underground. We stand on a platform by train tracks and wait for a train called the subway. We get off. Go up some stairs. We separate from *Marcella* and her husband. Their home is in another part of Toronto. We stand by another set of tracks and wait for another subway. We get off and go up some other stairs that eventually lead us outside. It is snowing. And it is cold. There is a wind that feels like a knife's edge across my face. I pull up the collar of my new coat to no effect. We wait at the corner for something called a streetcar, a short train that runs in the middle of the street. I follow in a daze, overwhelmed. Everything is so big: streets, sidewalks, buildings, cars, buses. Tall buildings. Short buildings. Store windows all decorated. People moving in every direction. I feel dizzy.

Toronto is a big city, not like *Sant'Elia*. I could not have imagined it. We have spent so much time on subways, streetcars, and buses, and all that time we never left Toronto! We're on the last stretch of our journey. Once we're off the bus, it's a "short" walk. But the intense cold and accumulated snow make it almost impossible to complete. The snow is so deep it fills my new boots, and my feet get wet. From head to toe I begin to feel numbness. In my coat pockets, my hands are frozen because I have no gloves. My ears ache and my head hurts because I have no hat. I'm afraid to breathe.

"*Eccola là, la casa.*" (There it is, the house.) *Zio Vincenzo* points out when our destination is within view. I quicken my step to escape the cold. The house is a bungalow. Rather than the front door, we go to the back. *Severino*, the owner of the house, greets us with a wide-open door and a loud, raspy voice. A temporary bottleneck at the entrance as we all shed our iced coats and shoes. Inside, it is surprisingly warm, thank God.

A New Beginning ...

CANADIAN IMMIGRATION IDENTIFICATION CARD

NAME	COCOROCCHIO Bruno
BIRTH (Day) (Month) (Year)	11 Dec 1951
PLACE AND COUNTRY OF BIRTH	Pontecorvo ITALY

SIGNATURE OF RIGHTFUL HOLDER

CANADA
87

THIS CARD, WHEN STAMPED BY A CANADIAN IMMIGRATION OFFICER, IS EVIDENCE THAT THE RIGHTFUL HOLDER IS A LANDED IMMIGRANT

THIS CARD IS REQUIRED FOR CUSTOMS CLEARANCE AND WHEN MAKING APPLICATION FOR CITIZENSHIP. IT WILL ALSO PROVE USEFUL FOR MANY OTHER PURPOSES.

FOR USE OF CARRIER
M/N "VULCANIA,,
ITALIAN LINE
NAPOLI HALIFAX

DEC 2 1964

IMM. 1000 (REV 3-64)

DATE AND PORT STAMP
CANADA IMMIGRATION
DEC 2 1964
HALIFAX, N.S.

1965 - Bruno, Mamma, Papà, Fulvia

CHAPTER 14

La Prima Abitazione
The First Abode

BEFORE WE COME TO CANADA, *PAPÀ* AND *ZIO VINCENZO* RENT the entire basement of a house in Scarborough, except for the *cantina*, a long, dark corridor under the staircase where *Severino*, the landlord, stores his demijohns, gallons, and bottles full of homemade wine. At the bottom of the stairs is our living room. There is a used black-and-white TV. To the left are the kitchen and dining areas. Across is a door that leads to the large bedroom where *Mamma e Papà* sleep, and a smaller bedroom for *Fulvia*. To the right of the staircase is a hallway that leads to the third bedroom that *Zio Vincenzo* and I share. This third bedroom is also used as a shop that houses a sewing machine *Papà* and *Zio Vincenzo* use to generate extra income. Each room is moderately furnished with essential secondhand furniture and appliances. I'm excited to have a TV and almost forget my disappointment of not getting a bedroom of my own. Also part of our rented space is a bathroom with a huge bathtub!

Zio Vincenzo is six years younger than *Papà*. He is also a tailor. He and *Papà* immigrated to Canada together, and he'll be living with us because he's not married. He has a *fidanzata* (fiancée) in *Sant'Elia* who might join him in the future. *Papà* and *Zio Vincenzo* work at the same clothing factory in downtown Toronto. *Papà* sews pant legs all day, and *Zio Vincenzo* assembles front panels of suit jackets. They call it "piece work." The more they do, the more they get paid.

Severino is a new friend. He's from *Sora*, a town not far from *Sant'Elia*. He is older than *Papà*. He and his wife, *Rosetta*, who is younger than *Mamma*, have been in Canada a long time. They have a son named *Alfredo* who is four years younger than me. The three of them live upstairs. *Severino* doesn't work because of some work-related accident. *Rosetta* is a lead-hand at a plastics factory in Scarborough. She says that she can get *Mamma* a job.

Friday, Saturday, and Sunday are a blur. From mid-afternoon on Friday until late Sunday night is one continuous celebration, or so it seems. *Papà* has made many friends in Canada. Some are new, and some are old acquaintances from *Sant'Elia*. Everyone has come to see and welcome us to Canada and ask about their relatives back in Italy. They toast to our future. They drink *Severino*'s wine and do shots of liquor from bottles that some have brought for the occasion. They sit around the kitchen table and talk and reminisce. Tired as she is, *Mamma* soon finds her role: to prepare and serve food to the visitors. As time passes, the conversations get louder. The more they drink, the more they talk. They tell jokes, some of them not meant to be heard by innocent ears. They laugh. Recount stories from the past. Boast achievements in the new world. I eat. Listen to their tales. Watch TV. Observe. Sleep.

Saturday morning when I get up, everyone is busy. The kitchen is clean and organized. *Mamma* is at the stove cooking. I smell the aroma from my bedroom. She has already been grocery shopping with *Rosetta*. *Papà* and *Zio Vincenzo* are outside helping

Severino clear a walkway of snow. I feel guilty for having slept in. In the afternoon, people start to arrive again; some are new, some we met yesterday. The drinking, talking, laughing continues.

Mamma is not happy, but *Papà* ignores her. He's always ready to have a drink with his new friends. He sits down at the table with them and orders *Mamma* to bring this and that. I can tell that she is angry by the side looks she gives him and his buddies. I wish *Papà* was more aware of *Mamma*'s feelings.

On Sunday, I wake up late again. *Severino* is chatting with *Papà* at the kitchen table and drinking espresso with *sambuca*. *Mamma* is busy at the stove. I smell the sauce she's making and my mouth waters. For *pranzo* we have my favorite pasta, *zitone*. I eat two platefuls! Then I eat a large piece of meat so tender that it melts in my mouth. *Mamma* still talks of her trip to the grocery store yesterday. She repeats that she never saw such beautiful produce anywhere! And in the month of December, mind you. Everything in that store was so fresh and perfect! Not as many visitors today.

After lunch, everyone disperses, except for *Mamma*. *Zio Vincenzo* announces that he is going *al cinema* downtown to see a movie. I imagine where he may be going and wish I could go too. I remember *'zappitt*, the cinema I used to go to in *Sant'Elia*. *Papà* moves from his seat at the table to the sofa chair in front of the TV. Soon he is asleep, snoring loudly. *Fulvia* disappears in her room to play with her doll, I guess. *Mamma* tells me to go to my room too. She stays in the kitchen to clean up. She must be tired. I wish for her to sit down and rest, but she says, "Who is going to do the work then? "*I so' semp stata e rèst' la schiava!*" (I have always been and always will be the slave) she whimpers to herself as she scrubs the pots and pans.

Mr. & Mrs. Rocco Cocorocchio
238 Lumsden Avenue
Toronto, Ontario, Canada

1966 - Papà   1966 - *Mamma*

1967 - Fulvia, Papà, Mamma

1967 - Papà

CHAPTER 15

Il Secondo Primo Giorno di Scuola
The Second First Day of School

IT'S MONDAY MORNING, THE START OF A NEW WEEK AND A NEW life. The alarm is set for 7:00 A.M. As I'm waking up, *Papà* and *Zio Vincenzo* are starting to work. They left at 5:30 A.M. to catch the 6:00 A.M. bus to go downtown. *Mamma* left with *Rosetta* at 6:30 A.M. to see if she can get a job at the plastics factory.

Fulvia and I have the breakfast *Mamma* laid out for us before she left. At 8:00 A.M., *Severino* calls from upstairs to check if we're ready to go. Last night, he agreed to take us to our new school to register. He knows the staff there because it's the same school his son goes to: St. Dunstan Catholic School. We go by side streets, as there is no transit. I hold *Fulvia's* hand, and together we follow *Severino*. Luckily, most sidewalks are clear of snow. My feet feel cold, but they're not wet. The school is a big redbrick building with a courtyard. Some kids are throwing a ball against the wall and catching it. They're all bundled up in puffy coats, woolen hats, boots, and gloves.

Severino goes directly to the front desk and explains to the secretary the purpose of our visit. Sister St. Ruth Maria, the principal of the school, invites us to her office. *Severino* then informs her of our situation. In Italy, I was enrolled in *la Terza Media*, the equivalent of Grade 8 in Canada. And *Fulvia* was enrolled in Grade 5. Now that we're in Canada, we'd like to continue in the same grades. The nun listens attentively, but from what I can surmise, because we don't speak English, she thinks that we would do better if we were both placed back a year. *Severino* argues that at least one of us should continue in the same grade, and that someone should be me because I've already been taught algebra, and Canadian students in the same grade have not. When he's ready to leave, *Severino* shakes the nun's hand and turns to me with a big grin that says, 'We did it, little man!'

I follow Sister St. Ruth Maria to my classroom, where she introduces me to my teacher. His name is Mr. MacDonald. She tries to tell him my name, but she has a hard time pronouncing it. Embarrassed, she goes back to her office. Mr. MacDonald looks at the piece of paper the nun has just given him and leads me to the front of the class. He introduces me and he, too, pronounces my name badly. Everyone in the classroom snickers. I don't understand why. He then takes me to an empty desk at the back of the room and returns to the front to continue teaching.

Every day from 8:30 A.M. to 3:00 P.M. I sit at my desk in the back of the classroom and draw pictures of villages under a blanket of snow. I miss the mountains that I stared at from the balcony of *Palazzo Gagliardi*. I've tried to follow Mr. MacDonald's lectures, but to no avail. The same applies to connecting with my classmates. They all seem to talk too fast. They appear to make no effort to help me understand them. They don't care. I feel frustrated. They continue to use words that I don't know. And when I frown, they mock me.

There are only two boys I can communicate with: *Alfredo* and *Silvio*. *Alfredo* is *Severino*'s son. *Fulvia* and I walk to school with him every day. He's in Grade 3 and was born in Canada. He speaks a little of his parents' dialect, which I barely understand. *Silvio*, on the other hand, speaks decent Italian. He's in Grade 7. Like me, he was born in Italy, but his parents brought him to Canada when he was two years old. He's very popular, especially with the girls. He acts as my translator. I like *Silvio*. At times, I wish that Sister St. Ruth Maria had placed me in Grade 7. Recess is the hardest part of my school day because the boys in the schoolyard ridicule how I look, what I wear, how I speak, and how I can't play their silly games. The playground at St. Dunstan's is where I learn to resent words like WOP, GOOMBAH, and DEGO.

One group of boys always taunts me. These youths stand out from the others in the way they dress and in the way they walk. They're always in a group of five or six. They wear blue jeans and denim jackets, even when it's very cold. Their leather boots are pointed. They look like the cowboys I've seen on TV, except for their hair and the fact that they don't wear hats. Instead, they fix their hair in a funny sort of way; from the back and sides of the head, the hair is slicked up into a channel on top that's then carefully funneled to hang in the middle of the forehead. The leader stands out because he has the most fastidious hairdo. I wear my hair short, so I could never replicate their style.

Today the group is particularly nasty towards me, and I lose control. I pin the leader of the gang to the ground, straddling his core and holding his wrists down with my hands. He kicks his legs and wiggles, but to no effect. I'm a ball of nerves, shaking with anger. I wish I could erase the picture in front of my eyes. I don't want to be part of it.

"*Eh, Bruno, cosa fai? Fermati. Lascialo stare.*" (Eh, Bruno, what are you doing? Stop. Let him be.) *Silvio* has come to my rescue. He begs me to stop and to let the leader go. I release my hold. My opponent quickly gets up and, before he and his buddies run away, kicks me in the shins with his pointy boot. I ignore the searing pain in my leg. I'm more concerned about the torn pocket in my coat and the ripped pant leg over my scuffed knee. How will I explain to *Mamma* what happened?

Fortunately, I get home before *Mamma* is back from the factory. I go straight to my room and inspect the tears on the overcoat and the pant leg. I clean, as best as I can, the scrape on my knee and check my face in the mirror for any scratches. I decide not to tell *Mamma* about the brawl. She wouldn't understand. If I told her, she'd get angry with me and then start crying. I'll tell *Papà* instead, or maybe *Zio Vincenzo*, tonight. I hope they can fix the rips and make them almost invisible. *Mamma e Papà* can't afford to buy me new clothes. I feel bad. I should have held back. I promise myself to never again get into a fight.

I often think about the friends I left behind in *Sant'Elia*. I miss them a lot. I wish they were here. I want them to see where I am and what I'm doing. I think about the girls in my old class. They're different from the Canadian girls. Here they look and smile at me, almost mischievously. At least that's how I interpret their smirks. I think I prefer them. Maybe it's because they have blonde hair, or maybe because they dress differently. And they're not shy. Some of them wear makeup too. I've picked a favorite. She has long blonde hair, a beautiful soft face, and is always very elegant, both in dress and mannerism. I imagine her as my girlfriend. And when I allow myself to daydream, she becomes my wife.

Time passes slowly in the back of the classroom. It is February. Sister St. Ruth Maria and Mr. MacDonald regularly discuss my progress, or lack thereof. The principal tries to teach me English. In the afternoons, I go to her office and we begin my lessons. Our lessons, actually. The Sister wants to learn Italian, so we trade: an apple for *una mela*, a table for *un tavolo*, and a chair for *una sedia*. At the end of March, my progress is negligible. My situation does not look good. Luckily, the principal finds a school that specializes in teaching basic English to immigrants, and she refers me there. On my first day, I get up early and go with *Papà* downtown, where the school is located. He shows me which streetcar to take and where to get off. I sit by the window, and *Papà* cracks it open a bit so I don't get sick. Tomorrow I will do this trip on my own because it's out of *Papà's* way. After a month of special classes, I score forty-nine out of fifty on a Grade 8 level English comprehension test. I am ready to go back to St. Dunstan's. It's the last week of May.

At the end of the school year, Mr. MacDonald has a choice. He can either make me repeat Grade 8 or pass me on to Grade 9. He chooses to promote me to high school. I am very happy, but sad too, because I'll no longer see my blond girlfriend. My Grade 8 report card is mostly blank except for what Mr. MacDonald wrote:

> *Because Bruno attended a special language school (COSTI) and received such good reports, and because of his obvious intent in learning English, I have graded him more in accord with his potentialities than in actual results obtained in the June exams.*
>
> *Good Luck, Bruno.*

By the end of August, we will have stayed in *Severino's* basement apartment for nine months. Now we are moving from Scarborough to a two-storey house in East York that *Papà* and *Zio Vincenzo* have bought together.

When I left St. Dunstan's, I was given the name of the high school I would be attending in September: Birchmount Park

Collegiate Institute. Now because we're moving, I have to switch schools. To determine which school I'm supposed to go to, I have to meet with an advisor at the East York Board of Education.

My appointment is at 2:30 P.M. I have all the documents I need: report cards, tests, certificates, and proof of address. I have the two transit tickets *Papà* gave to me last night, one for going and one for coming back. I review my transit instructions. At 1:00 P.M., I walk to the corner of Leyton Avenue and Danforth Avenue to board my bus.

I sit across from the guidance counselor as he reviews my file. He asks why I am applying for the five-year academic program and not the four-year vocational. "I want to go to university," I answer. He grimaces and then asks if I know how difficult the five-year program is. I repeat, "I want to go to university." He then goes on to explain that immigrants have a hard time just completing the four-year program. The five-year program would be that much more difficult. "You won't make it," he states disparagingly. He then continues to say that after completing Grade 12 I could easily get a job and start making money right away. My reply is, "I want to go to university. I need Grade 13." Reluctantly, he gives in to my request and enrolls me in the academic stream at Danforth Technical School, a school that offers both study choices. On the way home, I promise myself three things: one, to prove the counselor wrong; two, to study hard; and three, to go to university.

I imagine myself years in the future, coming back to that very same address. Meeting with that very same counselor who continues to sit behind that very same desk. Placing an elegantly framed university degree with my full name embossed in large black letters in front of him and saying, "You were so wrong, mister! Shame on you!"

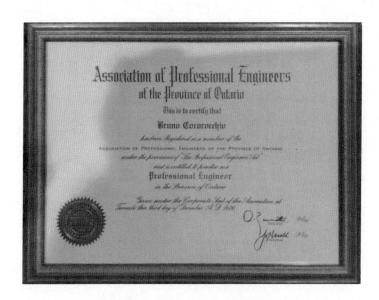

1976 – Bruno Cocorocchio, P. Eng.

CHAPTER 16

L'Asino di Lavoro
Beast of Burden

Mamma WAS EIGHT YEARS OLD WHEN WORLD WAR II BROKE OUT. It was then that she stopped going to school to become her mother's work mule. There was no one else available. *Mamma*'s older brother, *Fernando*, was apprenticing to become a carpenter. Her older sister, *Nina*, was living in Naples with a wealthy family as their housemaid. And at five months pregnant, *Nonna* wasn't able to manage working at the mill and looking after her two young boys, *Benito* and *Vincenzo*. *Mamma* was happy because she much preferred the outdoors to being cooped up inside a classroom. Caught in between siblings that were either too young to make a difference or old enough to be earning money for the family, *Mamma*'s plight was destined.

The war continued, the paper mill closed, and life in the village became increasingly harsh. In addition to her babysitting duties, and because she was sturdy and strong, *Mamma* was sent out with other townsfolk to collect firewood in the mountain forests. She left in the middle of the night and returned with a full load before her brothers were awake. Some afternoons, when *Benito* and *Vincenzo* were napping, on her own initiative,

Mamma ventured farther afield into soldiers' camps to beg for food. Usually she succeeded in gathering a few potatoes and carrots, an odd can of beans or tuna, and, if she was really lucky, a couple of pieces of chocolate. But no matter what her sack contained, when she got home, *Nonna* greeted her with a beating.

One such afternoon, *Mamma* returned home with something different, or so she thought. Something *Nonna* would appreciate. Something, perhaps, worthy of praise and not punishment. A soldier had entrusted her with a bag of dirty laundry that, if brought back clean, would fetch a good pay. And if the soldier didn't go away, it would mean a regular income for the household. Rather than praise, *Nonna* delivered a dose of her customary abuse. Used to this mistreatment, *Mamma* took it in stride without uttering a sound. Her contributions were continually glossed over. She learned to keep her festering emotions bottled up inside.

When the war finally ended, *Nonna* was a widow. Her last born, *Ettore*, was ready to start kindergarten. *Benito* and *Vincenzo* were sent to elementary school, and *Mamma* was to continue as her mother's work mule, *gliu' ciucc' p' fatià*. In addition to her household duties, she now was forced to look for work. She competed with older and more experienced men for the same job. She joined work crews as a day laborer and pushed wheelbarrows full of dirt and stones. Whatever she was paid at the end of the day she brought to her mother. She kept nothing for herself, except, perhaps, a growing resentment towards her siblings. *Nonna* was too busy to take notice.

Slowly, life returned to the town. Rubble was cleared away, homes were reestablished, and family members reunited. Young men sought work opportunities. Some started families of their own. Others learned new trades. *Nonna*'s family was no different.

Fernando, after completing his apprenticeship, immigrated to France. Following in his brother's footsteps, *Benito* also learned carpentry and, a few years later, joined his older brother. *Nina* stayed on in Naples and became an integral part of the family she served. After completing Grade 5, *Vincenzo* apprenticed in the same tailor shop where *Papà* worked. *Ettore* started elementary school. He would continue with his education to be the first in the family to go beyond fifth grade to obtain a diploma as an electro-mechanical technician. And *Mamma*? Well, *Mamma* continued as the family's work mule. She worked and worked. And she never voiced a complaint. If she had anything to say, she kept it to herself. In the spring of 1951, at almost twenty years old, *Mamma* left her mother's house and married *Papà*. She kept on working. At the end of that year, she gave birth to me. And she almost stopped working... forever.

There's a local proverb that adequately describes *Mamma's* predicament: *Attacca 'gliu ciucc addó vo 'gliu padrone* or *Attacca l'asino dove vuole il padrone* (Tie the donkey where the master wants). This saying symbolizes resignation and obedience. For most of her life, *Mamma* was the donkey. From early childhood onwards, she surrendered to a life of reverence and servitude. The war years and the fact that she was a middle child helped to solidify her low rank in society. Like a donkey, *Mamma* submissively absorbed the beatings she received from her mother without resistance, and she followed her mother's orders without hesitation.

Over time, she learned to bend under the increasing weight, to such an extent that she became dehumanized. Her so-called strength was to hold in rather than lash out. Growing up, I tried to emulate *Mamma's* fortitude. I took the punishments she afforded me, hoping to dissipate her internalized frustration.

However, I was too naive to know that there was nothing I could do for her. And after my beatings, I cried with her to show her that she wasn't alone. But again my innocence prevented me from realizing that I was a victim myself. Looking back, I sacrificed my childhood exuberance in pursuit of the unattainable: *Mamma*'s happiness.

It would be years later when I finally understood why *Mamma*, whenever she signed a document, would become flustered and apologize profusely. She would begin by positioning herself in front of the blank line and spread her elbows, anchoring them to the writing surface. Then she'd carefully hold the pen in her callused hand and slowly begin to write out the string of letters comprising her name, stopping to check her progress when she feared she had lost her place. The elongated signature would always exceed the allotted space: *E-L-E-N-A C-O-C-O-R-O-C-C-H-I-O.*

The first dozen years of *Mamma e Papà*'s life together did not produce tangible results. If anything, they became poorer after *Fulvia* and I were born. Parental obligation dictated looking for work outside of Italy. So, in 1964, when the opportunity presented itself by way of Canada, *Mamma e Papà* were as ready as could be. And for the thirty-plus years that followed, they worked long and hard to reach their ultimate goal—to prove to the world (or their respective brothers and sisters) that they could make it on their own.

Papà continued in the familiar tailoring trade, and *Mamma* carved out a new path for herself. She started working the same day she was introduced to the factory foreman where our landlady was working. After a brief demonstration, *Mamma* was planted in front of a machine that opened and closed automatically with barely enough time to pull out the molded form from a scorching oven. Over the decades that followed, mold shapes changed, machines were upgraded, and foremen reassigned, but *Mamma* remained the same. The burn scars up and down her arms became her identity badge as well as a time graph of the factory's evolution. Like a good workhorse, she followed instructions until the day she retired.

Whenever I complain about working too much, *Papà* reminds me of an old Italian proverb: *Il lavoro nobilita l'uomo*, or work ennobles man. *Mamma e Papà* were born to be workers, not only in *Sant'Elia* but also in Canada. When *Papà* arrived in Toronto, he had no money. He didn't speak English, and he had no one to help him with the transition from small-town Italy to big-city Canada. He had come to work, and work he sought. In no time, he found a job and a place to live. Three months later, he sent for the family he'd left behind. And with *Mamma*'s help, a year after he had set foot in Toronto, he was able to put a down payment on a house. The formula for their success was extremely simple: wake-up, go to work, come home, eat, go to sleep… then start over again.

Mamma, Papà, and *Zio Vincenzo* worked as many hours as they could at the factories. *Papà* and *Zio Vincenzo* left at 5:45 A.M., and if they didn't work a couple of hours of overtime, they returned home at six in the evening. *Mamma* did the 7:00 A.M. to 3:00 P.M. shift, and sometimes the 7:00 A.M. to 10:00 P.M. double shift. There was no quenching their appetite for work.

On weekends, *Papà* and *Zio Vincenzo* worked at home, making tailor-made suits for a developing clientele. *Mamma* took care of all the cooking, shopping, cleaning, and laundry. Typically, *Zio Vincenzo* went out on Sunday afternoons to the cinema. *Papà* and *Mamma* always stayed home. Some Fridays after work, *Papà* went with co-workers to a beer parlor. Sometimes they went to see naked dancers at a strip club downtown. On those nights when *Papà* came home, he and *Mamma* argued. They followed a familiar pattern: *Papà* arrives feeling jovial; *Mamma* greets him with reprimands; *Papà* raises his voice; *Mamma* continues her chiding. The bickering escalates. Finally, *Papà's* belligerence reaches a peak, and *Mamma* becomes hysterical. Referring to *Severino* and *Rosetta* upstairs she pleads, "Don't yell, you'll wake up the whole neighborhood!"

I am allowed to watch TV, but only after I have completed my schoolwork. I watch the same TV shows every day: *Gilligan's Island* and *Bewitched*. With the repeated watching, I begin to recognize words, comprehend dialogue, and follow the plot of the stories. Over time, I'm able to transfer that skill to real-life conversations and soon take on the role of resident translator. I understand much more than I will verbalize. I hold back because I don't want to sound like another Italian speaking English with a heavy accent. I don't want to give the kids at school any more reason to make fun of me. When I speak, I will sound just like them. With no accent.

With *Severino's* help, I prepare the first Canadian income-tax returns for *Mamma e Papà* and, a day later, for *Zio Vincenzo*. After about four months in Canada, this is the first time my knowledge of the English language is tested. Because they each have only one source of employment income to report, the preparation of the returns isn't too difficult. As for the cash money

Papà and *Zio Vincenzo* earned from the suits they made in their spare time, *Severino* says, "The government doesn't know what it doesn't know."

Each package contains a worksheet. Using a pencil, I begin with *Papà*'s return. Attentively, I follow *Severino*'s guidance in Italian to decipher the corresponding step in the government-issued instructions, as well as connect to the appropriate box on the income statement. I transcribe numbers from the statement to the worksheet. I use a blank sheet of paper to add and subtract figures, double-check my arithmetic before transposing the final result to the appropriate line on the form. When I have completed the process and announce the result, everyone is happy because my calculations show that the government owes *Papà* money. I then follow the same procedure to complete *Mamma*'s return. She too has money coming back, but not as much as *Papà*. She is disappointed, as if she has lost a competition. *Zio Vincenzo* says that he will do his own return. Next day, however, he asks me to do it, with the added promise, "I'll take you to the cinema on Sunday." I wish it was Sunday already!

1940s - Refugees return to what is left of their homes.

1940s - Ascent from the *Rapido* to the town of *Sant'Elia Fiumerapido*

1960s – Ascent from the *Rapido* to the town of *Sant'Elia Fiumerapido*

1940s – *Zia Anna (Zio Fernando's* wife), *Mamma, Zia Nina*

2010s – *Mamma* works while *Papà* rests

CHAPTER 17
Tornare Indietro
Going Back

IN 2001, AFTER THIRTY-SEVEN YEARS IN CANADA, *MAMMA E PAPÀ* moved back to Italy. She was seventy; he was seventy-three. Since then, I've visited them regularly—usually unaccompanied and typically for three weeks. The purpose of each visit is always the same: to assuage my never-ending guilt.

The apartment my parents have bought is situated in the outskirts of town, not far from where *Nonna* used to live—down in the *Rapido* valley on a road that runs parallel to the river and leads to the cemetery.

The house is a duplex, a two-story structure with an apartment on each floor and two completely separate entrances. A younger couple occupies the apartment below. In addition to the top-floor apartment boasting a terrace that faces the town, *Mamma e Papà's* property includes a front garden with tropical plants, a back orchard with fruit trees, and a long driveway that connects the front to the rear and leads to an attached garage in the rear of the building. Various means are used to delineate ownership and separateness. Lockable gates at driveway entrances. Stone walls and iron rails around the garden. And mesh fencing at the orchard.

To access their apartment, *Mamma e Papà* follow a path that's not at all age-friendly. Through the front gate, along the edge of the garden down the driveway, up three steps to a landing. Through the outer front door. Up two flights of marble stairs to arrive at the second-floor landing. Through the inner front door to a hallway that accesses various living areas: the terrace, the kitchen, the dining/living room, the master bedroom with a walk-out balcony, the guest bedroom, the bathroom, and a doorway that leads through an iron spiral staircase to an unfinished attic.

For security purposes, *Mamma e Papà* employ three levels of protection: a single outer layer and a double inner layer. The outer layer comprises the lockable iron gate that separates the road from their driveway. This entry point is unlocked in the morning and locked at night and each time they leave the premises. For the inner layer, there is the outer front door. It automatically locks to the outside and, at night, is bolt-locked from the inside. Finally, there is the inner front door at the top of the staircase. This throughway is locked from the inside every night.

I have asked what would happen in case of an emergency. If, for example, one of them needed an ambulance in the middle of the night. In response, they change the subject. They prefer to not discuss it. With me.

When they took possession, the apartment wasn't to the same living standard *Mamma e Papà* had become accustomed while in Canada. Wasting no time, they got to work right away. The kitchen underwent a total makeover. The electrical system was upgraded, as was the plumbing. The bathroom was re-tiled. A fresh coat of paint was added throughout. Outside, the driveway was dug up and stone-paved. The garden was almost a replica of one of those pristine front lawns found in Canada in the summer. The orchard, weeded. The fruit trees, pruned. The vegetable garden, tilled. The fences, mended. The area at the back of the house was also transformed. Not needing a garage, the space was converted to *Mamma*'s rustic kitchen and *Papà*'s cellar. Well, cellar may be stretching it, but this is where *Papà* keeps his store-bought gallons of wine—it's cheaper this way, he says—and an array of empty vermouth bottles. He's often found here, transposing the *Montepulciano* from gallons to bottles for daily consumption.

Most of the work was carried out during the first year—ironically with help from *Roberto*, the nephew *Papà* had trained so long ago to become a tailor. A nurse now, *Roberto* played a key role in employing and negotiating with local tradespeople for his uncle.

Mamma e Papà do not like to be indebted. So for his time and effort, *Roberto* was lavishly compensated. In addition to cash payments, and to punctuate a certain accomplishment or job completion, *Mamma* would often slave from morning till night to deliver an elaborate meal for him and his family: wife, sons, and grandsons. My parents' way of entertainment became the talk of the town, and soon long forgotten friends and relatives started dropping by, hoping for an invitation to the next gathering.

These feasts would usually entail many homemade dishes served with copious amounts of wine. After each gathering, *Mamma* complained relentlessly to *Papà*. Her remarks would be directed primarily to the women at her table. How they just sat there and expected to be served. How their husbands didn't say a word. How she, the perennial workhorse, was expected to do everything. Like a slave. And did *Papà* not see the mountain of dishes she was left with? And did he not know that she was up at 4:00 A.M. to knead the dough for the homemade pasta? For the pizza that everybody devoured? And did he not notice how the son and his *fidanzata* behaved at the table? Just like swine, they were. And the parents just let it all go.

Whether with blood relations or relative strangers, all the relationships my parents developed were short-lived. During my frequent visits over the years, I would often hear stories of how this nephew had distanced himself for no apparent reason. Or how another acquaintance had stopped visiting them and was no longer returning calls. Or how so and so had been walking in their direction and suddenly crossed the road to avoid them. According to *Mamma e Papà*, they had done nothing wrong. The fault was always directed at the other people. So, over time, their circle of friends shrunk dramatically.

When I call from Canada, *Mamma* often recites the same litany of complaints. She is tired of being isolated. Of not being close to her children and grandchildren. That no one visits them like they used to. Unless, of course, there is a meal to be had. That she practically has to beg this cousin or that acquaintance for a ride to the grocery store, even when they're well compensated for their trouble. She curses *Papà* for moving back to Italy. For not learning how to drive. For not helping her. And how she wishes she was back in her cozy little bungalow in East York.

Over the years, the frequency of my trips to Italy has increased, as have my parents' age and frailty. The older they get, the harder it is to converse with them. *Papà* has lost most if not all of his hearing. *Mamma* has become more cantankerous. At the end of each visit, I am exhausted and more than ready to return home. I sense that they're happy to see me go. It's been difficult for them too, although they'd never admit it. As I drive to the airport, I review the weeks gone by and arrive at a familiar conclusion: to visit less often and shorten the time I spend with them when I do visit. These promises I make to myself, but never keep.

2016 - *Papà*'s Wine Cellar

CHAPTER 18
Ribellarsi Senza Voce
Rebel without a Voice

It is the sixteenth of December, 2004. It has been three-and-a-half years since *Mamma e Papà* moved back to Italy. This is their first return visit to Canada, their home for thirty-seven years. They've come to celebrate the holiday season with us, my sister and me. Their stay is two-and-a-half weeks. Half of that time, Christmas Eve and Christmas Day included, they will spend with me in Markham, and the other half, including New Year's Eve and New Year's Day, they will spend with my sister in Whitby.

My son and I have come to meet them at Toronto Pearson International Airport. The plane landed on time, at 9:30 p.m., over an hour ago. The bulk of passengers have come through. I wonder why it's taking them so long. The doors open and close. I stretch my neck as if to look for them around corners. Finally, I see *Mamma*. Then, slightly behind her, to her right, I see *Papà*. She looks irritated. He, somewhat oblivious. As soon as our gazes connect, she releases some of her tension. Even from a distance, I can tell what mood she's in. Always on the verge of tears, she informs me that "All of this, I suffer for you! I want you to know that!" When we are close, I ask why it took so long for them to come out. With clenched teeth, she answers by cursing the customs officer for wanting to inspect their luggage. "He was looking for the whore that is his mother!" We hug awkwardly.

Papà has his own particular greeting. He grabs my face with both hands, then squeezes and kisses me on both cheeks, making it impossible for me to return the greeting. We walk to the car. The two of them argue about who is to sit in the front seat with me. "You sit in the front. You've got the bad legs." "No, you sit in the front with your son! You're older." "No. You sit!" *Mamma* wins by saying she'd rather sit with her grandson. It's funny how *Mamma* always gets her way, even though she makes you feel sorry for her. I wonder why that is. Once settled in, it becomes quiet except for the tick-tick-tick of the turn signal of the car. I wind my way out of the airport and onto the freeway. In forty-five minutes, we should be at our destination.

Looking back, 2004 was quite the year for me. At the beginning, I am a married man. By spring, I am a desperate man. By summer, I am a resigned man. By fall, I am a confident man. And by year's end, I am an angry man.

In April of 2004, my third wife left me. She and I had been having problems for a while. The year before, she had left me twice, the first time for a week. She needed time alone, she said. The second time, she left for two months. She needed time away from me and *my* son. She needed time to reflect, she added. She took Teddy, our German shepherd, with her. She rented a room in a house in west Toronto without my knowing it. I knew she was close to her limit and that it was too late to turn things around. To be fair, she had stood by me for a long time.

Through many hardships. When we first met, I was in the midst of divorcing the mother of my son. She supported me during the fiercely contested negotiation phase. Then, when my wife suddenly died in a car crash, she accepted the fact that now our burgeoning relationship must include my ten-year-old son. She hadn't planned on having children, but she accepted mine. Together, we navigated his tumultuous teenage years. Then, if that hadn't been enough, there was the abrupt end of my corporate career followed by a costly failed attempt at retail. So, yes, she had a limit. And she had reached it. So it wasn't surprising to come home that dreary April evening and find the note that said, "Bruno, don't bother pursuing me. I am filing for divorce. You'll hear from my lawyer." We had lasted twelve years.

An old friend from high school suggested I join Lavalife, an online dating site. Mesmerized, I spent hours examining profiles of both men and women before I created one of my own and gathered enough courage to post it. My nickname was SEEK_H_ER, and my opening line was, "Lookin' for that certain spark ... are you?"

Especially intriguing were the replies and requests that ensued. One afternoon in July, there I was, flipping through pages of new postings, when I thought I had come across a familiar face. I stopped and looked at it closely. Can it be her? I wondered. To satisfy my curiosity, I sent out an introductory greeting to see if the recognition was mutual. The next day, I received a negative response. I let it go. However, later that afternoon, I was drawn back to the same profile. It was she; I was sure. This time, I offered a little more information to trigger the connection. The response was almost immediate. "Oh my God! I don't believe it! Yes, it's me, Bruno. I've often thought about you. Call me. And yes, I want to go to the movies with you." I was right. I called her, and in less than an hour, she was knocking at my door. Purely by chance, I had discovered the profile of the girl who had lived two doors up from my parents' house in East York. Thirty-five years ago.

At first, we are a boy and a girl who live next door to one another. Occasionally, we ride the bus together to our respective part-time jobs. After completing high school, I go to university to study engineering. She takes to the skies to become a flight attendant. I continue living with my parents. She ventures out on her own. A couple of years pass. She comes back to the old neighborhood. I see her as she steps out of her red convertible. She says, "Let me take you for a ride." I envy your freedom, is my inward reply. At her apartment, she offers me a drink.

For a time, we lose track of each other. Decades pass before we meet again. When we do, we both agree that it must be destiny. She lives in a house in East York with her two sons, ten and nineteen. I live in the suburbs with my twenty-one-year-old. We are both weary, lonely, and longing. She listens compassionately to my story and promises to never do like those other women have done. She will not abandon me. All she asks in return is for me to be her "soft landing." "I can do that," I assure her.

I break the silence by going over the plans I've made for the next few days. After a day of rest, we'll go to my parents' old neighborhood and knock on some doors to see if any of their old friends are still around. As promised, I will take *Mamma* to her favorite stores. The Italian grocer on the Danforth. The Dollar Store in Scarborough. And, as she specifically requested, to Honest Ed's, Toronto's world-famous discount store. Most important, however, is our trip to the Kensington fish market, where we'll buy the octopus for the traditional Christmas Eve dinner. Although not very enthusiastic, *Mamma e Papà* concur with the general outline.

I then think of the arrangements I've made for Christmas Eve and Christmas Day. I feel apprehensive about sharing them. Why? Because I haven't told them that my new friend has practically moved in with me, or that she and her sons are included in the Christmas celebrations. So what's wrong with telling them now? Because I'm afraid. I expect rejection. Disapproval. Denial. There. I've said it. A fifty-three-year-old man seeking his parents' permission. Ridiculous, is it not? A wave of anger invades my body. I want to yell out, "Enough already! Will I ever grow up? Unlikely. Yes, I take full responsibility. And yes, I am afraid of upsetting my dear *Mamma e Papà!*"

I linger on the Christmas Eve dinner and tell *Mamma* how much I'm looking forward to the octopus. It's been a long time. This year, I tell her, she must teach me the recipe. Then I begin to address the attendees to both dinners, Christmas Eve and Christmas Day. There will be thirteen in total. I start with my sister's family. Four, including her son's girlfriend. The two of them, of course. My son and his girlfriend. And, finally, five more, with me and my "new" friend's family. I tentatively go on describing who this friend is … I remind them of their old house … the black family that lived two doors up from us … how this new friend and I have recently reconnected … where she lives … about her sons … and finally, that she has become part of my life … that, sometimes, she stays overnight at my house. And … nothing. That is all. In response I get silence. An interminable silence.

Then *Papà* clears his throat loudly. He has something to say. A rehearsed speech, I fear. "Bru, we have spent a lot of money. Your mother and I have come all this way to be with our family. To celebrate these holidays with you and your sister. And with our grandchildren. This is our family. Do you understand? Not with strangers." Then silence, again. A lump rises from the pit of my stomach to the top of my throat, and blood rushes to my head. The internal scream reawakens. And nothing. Just more silence. I try hard to control myself. To formulate a response devoid of emotion. And, with colossal effort, I manage to say, "To my house, I invite who I want."

In deadening silence, I continue the drive home. I am thankful that my friend is at her house tonight and not mine. What a scene that would have made. I hear *Mamma*'s muted whimpering in the back seat. I park the car in the driveway. I get out and open the front door to the house. The three of them remain in the car, motionless, except for their grandson. He looks at *Mamma*, then at *Papà*. Avoids my gaze. I open the trunk and remove their suitcases. Still no movement from any of them. I ask why they're not getting out. Between snivels, *Mamma* mumbles something like, "We're not wanted here… What have we done, *Rucchi*? We should have stayed home! What do we do now, *Rucchi*? If we could just get back on that plane and pretend none of this ever happened… We are cursed, I tell you!" Exasperated, I direct my son to help bring the luggage in the house. I tell *Mamma e Papà* to stop the silliness and to get in the house where it's warm.

They sit, side-by-side, on the sofa in the living room. It's the closest seating to the front door. They have not taken off their coats or shoes. It is late. I suggest we all go to bed and postpone any discussion until next morning. *Papà* nods. In agreement? I'm not sure. I show them to their room. My son has brought the luggage. He has retreated to his room. I picture him on the phone to his girlfriend, reporting. And, at the same time, listening through his door. I'm aware of suppressing the anger within. I wish the miserable duo a good night's sleep and, exhausted, retire to my bedroom.

It's 7:00 A.M. I turn on the shower, and a rush of cold water hits my face. As I wait for the water to warm up, I relive last night's series of events. I wonder if they slept. How? A wave of anger surges through my veins. I throw on a pair of sweats and go down to the kitchen to put on some coffee. I find both seated at the table. They are wearing the same clothes as yesterday. Their faces are expressionless. They have not slept at all. *Papà* speaks. He informs me that they have spoken to my sister. Her husband is on his way to get them. They will stay with her. It's obvious that they're not wanted in my house. I could have told them that before they decided to visit. They will discuss with my sister how to proceed. Finally, he apologizes for any inconvenience they may have caused me.

That's it! Decision made. No discussion. No explanation. No compromise. At 8:00 A.M. sharp, my brother-in-law knocks at my door. A brief greeting. A quick loading of the yet-to-be-opened luggage. A curt goodbye. And they are gone.

A fury engulfs every cell of my body. Each cell is charged to explode. But nothing happens. Nothing has ever happened. No fireworks. No blowouts. Rage advances without respite and fizzles through the pores of my skin.

Why am I not surprised? Because I have been made to feel this way my entire life. They have always criticized me. Ridiculed me. Belittled my every accomplishment. Chastised my every action, good or bad. So why the anger now? Because now I am finally able to glimpse this behavior of theirs and recognize it for what it actually is. Abusive and controlling. But why be angry? Because I find myself with no audible voice. My tongue, strait-jacketed. Because my loudest scream is that of silence.

Those two-and-a-half weeks at the end of 2004 became the catalyst that separated me from my parents, specifically my mother. Our umbilical cord was finally severed. It wasn't an amicable undertaking. They didn't give up control without resistance. Actually, they never conceded defeat. As far as they were concerned, from the day I was born until the day they died, they had done nothing wrong. Whatever they had done was for my benefit. Every sacrifice they made was for my betterment. They had always stood there for me and took over for me when I was otherwise occupied or distracted.

The fact that they had suffered. Sacrificed for me. It is typical behavior. Theirs. And mine. They have controlled me my entire life and continue to do so. And I continue to let them. Even though I am fifty-three years old, I continue to be under their influence. And I continue to bend to their will. *Not this time!* I tell myself. This time I will not cave into them. I will actively reject their ever-familiar phrases that pierce my shield. Without clemency. Without pity. While they blame me for the damage they cause. And absolve themselves of any wrongdoing with the feeble excuse that they have sacrificed their lives for my welfare. For me, the ever-ungrateful son that I am. Inside my head, I am hosting a fiery debate. It's me against them. I have prepared my defense. I have rehearsed my speech. I am ready to present it. Except there is no one there to present it to. Everyone has gone home. No one cares about what I have to say.

Yes, now that they're gone, I wish I could have an audience to defend myself. To accuse them. Someone else but me. Instead, I am left alone to ruminate in my own poison. I go over what transpired since last night and start to think that, perhaps, I should have left my lover out of the equation. That I should have negotiated her out of the Christmas gatherings with my family. I should have given her the benefit of the doubt. She would have understood. Or would she? Why should she? Is she not my companion? Is she not the same as everybody else? Are they discriminating? Are they racists? Am I? What the fuck!? Of course, no line of reasoning led to an acceptable result. No. I wish my parents had stayed where they were. In their rat hole, in Italy! Why the fuck were they here, anyway? To raise hell. That is all!

What happened after they left? Did I see them again? Yes, I saw them again. I wish I hadn't, though. I did host a Christmas dinner after all. Of sorts. Without Mamma's participation. It was to keep some kind of peace, except no one was at peace. The whole group—*Mamma e Papà*, my sister, her husband, their son and his girlfriend, my son and his girlfriend, my lover and her two sons, the older with his girlfriend (yes, why not?)—came together under my roof. Once. How did it go? Terribly. The tension was so thick you could have cut it with a knife. A wake would have been more enjoyable! Yes, I maintained contact with them. A couple of times. Yes, I initiated the calls. All very brief. Once to wish them a Merry Christmas. Curiosity got the best of me, I suppose. I wanted to find out what they were up to. As for their return to Italy, I can only assume that they left on the third of January, as scheduled. I have a letter from them, dated January 5, 2005, that I received on February 1. Please see below.

The letter is the only significant piece of writing I possess of my father that is addressed specifically to me. I have kept it for posterity. As a record. In his broken Italian, he admonishes me for disrespecting him/them. He places all blame for the fallout squarely on my shoulders. He needed just "a few lines" to say what he/they had to say to me. He left it up to me to fix what I had created, if I so desired.

I have also included my terse reply to his short letter. In it, I attempt to disentangle the anger that has spread like a cancer to every part of my body and that I could not give voice to. Perhaps somewhat repetitious, but I needed to vent. To be heard. This was the first time I allowed myself to declare without restraint the malignancy that has been festering my entire life. I don't know if they read it or if they understood any of it. It was never mentioned. What I found out many years later is that they kept my letter. I discovered it amongst the "important papers" I had to sort through at the end of their lives.

The aftermath of that infamous return visit to Canada in 2004 was isolation. For more than two years, *Mamma e Papà* relinquished their dependence on me by keeping me out of their affairs. But they didn't forgo the opportunity to run interference in my domain. My sister and her husband took my place as their representatives, and they were also encouraged to take my place where my son was concerned. As a result, he and I suffered a separation. He left my house to go live with my sister while *Mamma e Papà* provided financial support. They encouraged him to hurt me, deeply. They knew my vulnerability and they accessed it. Without pity.

I wish I could say, "Fuck it!" and turn my back on the past. My parents. My mother. But I could not. And cannot. I don't know how. I envy those who rebel against fathers. Who break down barriers. Who ignore authority. And I admire those who follow their dreams. I applaud their courage, for I am spineless. Wingless. Speechless.

Letter from Italy, dated January 5, 2005.

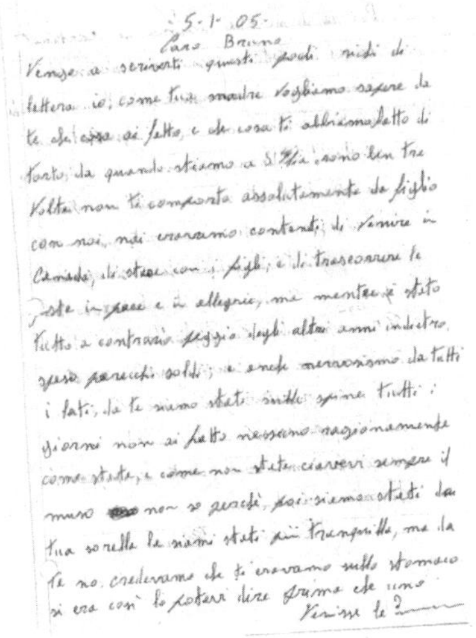

5-1-05
Caro Bruno
Vengo a scriverti questi pochi righi di
lettera io, come tua madre vogliamo sapere da
te che cosa ai fatto, e che cosa ti abbiamo fatto di
torto, da quando stiamo a St. ... sono ben tre
volte non ti comporta assolutamente da figlio
con noi, noi eravamo contenti di venire in
Canada, di stare con i figli, e di trascorrere le
feste in pace e in allegria, ma invece è stato
tutto a contrario peggio degli altri anni indietro,
speso parecchi soldi; e anche nervosismo da tutti
i lati, da te siamo stati sulle spine tutti i
giorni non ai fatto nessuno ragionamento
come stata, e come non state ciavevi sempre il
muso [illegible] non so perché, poi siamo stati da
tua sorella lì siamo stati più tranquilli, ma da
te no credevamo che ti eravamo sullo stomaco
si era così lo potevi dire prima che uno
Venisse te ...

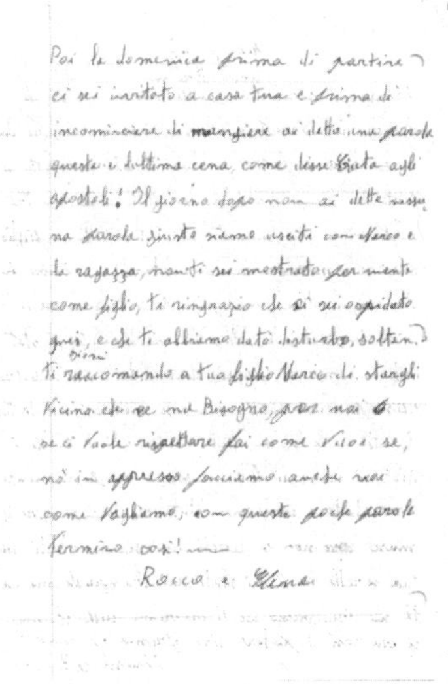

Poi la domenica prima di partire
ci sei invitato a casa tua e prima di
incominciare di mangiare ai detto una parola
questa è l'ultima cena, come disse Cristo agli
apostoli! Il giorno dopo non ai detto nessu-
na parola giusto siamo usciti con Marco e
la ragazza, non ti sei mostrato per niente
come figlio, ti ringrazio che ci sei ospitato
qui, e che ti abbiamo dato disturbo, soltan-
giorni
ti raccomando a tuo figlio Marco di stargli
vicino che se ne bisogno, per noi ...
se ci vuole rispettare fai come vuoi se,
no in appresso facciamo anche noi
come vogliamo, con queste poche parole
termino così!
Rocco e Gina

5 - 1 - 05

Dear Bruno

I come to write these few lines I, as well as your mother want to know from you what you have done, and what wrong we have done to you, from when we came back to Sant'Elia it has been three times that you have absolutely not behaved as a son with us, we were happy to come to Canada, to stay with our son and daughter, and to spend the holidays in peace and gaiety, but instead it has all been to the contrary worse than past years, spent lots of money; and also nervousness from all the facts, with you we were on thorns every day you showed no interest in how we were feeling, or not feeling you were always upset I don't know why, then we stayed with your sister there we were more calm, but not with you, we felt like we were sitting on your stomach if it was so you could have told us before we came there? ...

Then the Sunday before we leave you invited us to your house and before starting to eat you said a word *this is the last supper*, just as Judas said to the apostles! The day after, you did not utter a word we just went out with Marc and his girl, you did not behave at all like a son, I thank you for hosting us those days, and that we have disturbed you, I only hope you to look after your son Marco to stay near him 'cause he needs it, as for us, if you want to respect us, do as you please if not, in the future we will also do as we please, with these few words I end so! ...

Rocco and Elena

Letter from Canada, dated February 4, 2005.

MEA CULPA

1-2-4 Febbraio, 2005

Caro papà e mamma,

Oggi (il primo Febbraio) ho rcevuto la vostra tanta anticipata lettera... pensa un po'... una lettera scritta il 5 Gennaio e ricevuta l'1 Febbraio!

Da una parte, mi aspettavo una lettera forse piena di... critiche... sentenze... colpe.

Dall'altra parte, e forse quella più desiderata da me, mi aspettavo una lettera piena di scuse... giustificazioni ... spiegazioni... perdoni... collegamenti. Invece, la lettera che avete sritto non è ne l'una, e ne l'altra. Pare che vi scusate di tutto quel che è successo, e che date la colpa a me. Cioè, mi chiedete di voler sapere cosa io ho fatto, e che cosa mi avete fatto voi di torto a me.

Tu papà, hai scritto pochi righi— io, invece, cercherò di srivervi poche pagine... per forse così rispondere alle vostre tante domande.

Mi dite che il mio comportamento da figlio non è come quel che voi desiderate.

Pare che io sia un figlio piuttosto ingrato. Un figlio che non dimostra rispetto...

1-2-4 February 2005

Dear *Papà e Mamma,*

Today (1st of February) I received your most anticipated letter... just think... a letter written January 5 and received February 1!

On the one hand, I was expecting a letter perhaps full of... criticisms... verdicts... blame. On the other hand, and perhaps the one most desired by me, I was expecting a letter full of... excuses... justifications... explanations... forgiveness... reconnections. Instead, the letter you have written is not one or the other. It seems to me that you absolve yourselves of all that transpired by giving me total blame. That is, you ask me if I specify to you what it is that I have done, and what it is that you have done against me.

You, *Papà*, have written a few lines. I will try to write to you a few pages instead... to hopefully answer your so many questions.

You tell me that my behavior as a son is not what you wish of me. That, apparently, I am an ungrateful son.

A son that does not show respect...

che non riconoscie ciò che voi avete speso per venire a trovarci per venire a rivedere il vostro Canada per venire a trascorrere le feste con i vostri figli.

Etc. Etc.

Queste critiche non sono nuove critiche per me. Invece, sono una continuazione di critiche che mi avete fatto ... forse da quanto son nato. Sempre critiche. Sempre rimproveri. Sempre colpe.

Forse per difendermi, io potrei ben dire che, la maggior parte delle vostre critiche non siano vere ... che non siano giustificate ... che non siano mie. Ma, noi ben sappiamo, che non ne vale il fiato.

Quello che ho pensato ... quello che ho sentito io ve l'ho già detto parecchie volte in persona la volta più recente, uno o due giorni dopo il vostro arrivo in Canada.

Chiarisco ... dopo che voi avete espresso i vostri pensieri - pensieri e piani già fatti prima dell'arrivo in Canada - prima dell'arrivo nella mia casa.

E pure qui, voi volete/potete scusarvi, e dare la colpa a me, per non aver detto niente! Ma che cosa dovevo dirvi?

... that does not appreciate the money you spent to come visit us ... to come back for a visit to *your Canada* ... to come and spend the holidays with your son and daughter. Etc., etc.

These criticisms are not new criticisms for me. Rather, they are a continuation of the criticisms you have given me ... from the day I was born. Always critical. Always reproachful. Always guilty.

Perhaps in my defense I could say that the majority of your blame has no basis ... that it is not justifiable ... that it does not belong to me. But, as we well know, this denial would be a waste of breath.

What I have thought ... what I have felt ... I have told you many times already, in person ... most recently, one or two days after your arrival in Canada.

Let me clarify ... after you expressed your thoughts and plans that you had already decided prior to arriving in Canada— prior to entering my home.

And even here, you wish to absolve yourselves and blame me for not saying anything to you. But what is it that I am to say to you?

MEA CULPA

*Da parte mia, io mi son sentito
offeso ... voi, con i vostri giudizii
già premedidati, mi avete offeso. E
questa, come voi ben sapete, non è
stata la prima volta!*

*Voi fate quel che fate, e vi scusate
con la ragione che voi siete i
genitori ... che voi siete coloro che
hanno sacrificato tutta la loro vita
per i loro figli. Voi date sempre la
colpa a chi se la vuole prendere.*

*Nel passato, sono stato sempre io a
prendermela, e a fare quel che ho
potuto fare, per ripagarvi i vostri
sacrifici. Voi mi dite che non capite
come io la penzi, e come io agisco
il fatto è che, non mi avete mai
capito, e non mi avete mai sentito.*

*Nella vostra lettera voi dite che sono
tre anni ormai ... da quando siete
ritornati in Italia ... che a voi,
pare che io sia cambiato ... che voi
non capite cosa mi sta succedendo
ebbene, l'unica cosa che è successo
tra noi, è che ora c'è una certa
lontananza entro noi trè.*

*Con questa lontanaza, c'è stata una
certa diminuzione dell'obligo che
ho sempre sentito verso di voi. Della
colpa che ho sempre accettato e
portato come debito verso di voi.*

For my part, I have felt
offended ... you, with your
premeditated prejudices, have
offended me. And this, as you
well know, is not the first time!

You do what you do and excuse
yourselves because you are
the parents ... those who have
sacrificed your entire lives for us,
your children. You always give
fault to those who are willing to
take it.

In the past, I have accepted this
blame and done whatever I could
to repay you for your sacrifices.
You tell me that you don't
understand the way I think, how
I act ... the fact is that you have
never understood me, and you
have never heard me.

In your letter you write that it's
been three years already ... since
your return to Italy ... that to
you, I appear to have changed ...
that you don't understand what
may be happening to me ... well,
the only thing that has happened
to us is that now there is a certain
distance that separates us three.

With this distance, there has
been a certain reduction in the
obligations I have always held
towards you. Of the guilt I have
always accepted and carried as my
debt to you.

*Un obligo e una colpa che non
sono stati mai miei che però voi
mi avete sempre dato in gran
quantità. Con la lontananza, pare
che il mio peso—obligo e colpa—si
sia alleggerito.*

*Al principio, mi siete veramente
mancati—e fù per quel manca-
mento che io e Catherine venemmo
in Italia a trovarvi... dopo quei
tre o quattro mesi—per vedere,
con i miei occhi, come stavate. Noi
pure spesimo parecchi soldi, per un
accolto da voi alquanto freddo e
piuttòsto, inospitabile!*

*Sono anni e anni che cerco di capire
quel che io sento verso di voi due.*

*Che ho forse sentito verso di voi,
tutta la mia vita—ma, che fino
a recentemente, non ci ho dato
tanto peso.*

*In contemplazione però, vedo una
mia vita piena di critiche continue,
e di disprezzi. Fin da piccolo,
non ricordo un'occasione dove voi
mi avete incoraggiato, accettato e
moralmente aiutato.*

*Per quel che ero... per quel che mi
succedeva per quel che io vivevo per
quel che io facevo per quel che il
mio destino mi offriva... voi siete
sempre stati inconsapevoli e critici.*

A duty and accusation that have
never been mine... but that you
always have given me in bulk.
With distance, it now appears
that my burden—guilt and
blame—has decreased in weight.

In the beginning, I truly missed
you, and it was to fill that void
that Catherine and I came to
visit you... after those three four
months... to see, with my own
eyes, how you were coping. We
too spent much money for a most
cold and inhospitable reception
from the two of you. But even
here, you excuse yourselves... and
blame me... is that not true?

It has been years that I have tried
to understand what it is that I feel
towards you two. That perhaps I
have felt towards you my whole
life—but that, until recently,
I never gave much weight/
thought to.

In contemplation, however, I
see my life full of criticism and
deprecation. From when I was
a little boy, I have no memory
of a time when you encouraged
me, when you accepted me and
morally helped me.

For what I was... for what was
happening to me... for what was
my life... for what I was doing...
for what my destiny offered me...
you have always been critical
and unaware.

*Quel che io ricordo, è sempre
d'avere avuto un obbligo verso
voi due ... un obligo di dover
contracambiare la mia felicità, con
i vostri sacrifici.*

*Esempii ce ne sono parecchi—da
quanto ero piccolo (vi ricordate la
famosa bicicletta ch'era mia e non
era mia), a poche settimane fà (con
la rinunzia di Darlene).*

*Durante quest'ultima occasione,
cioè il vostro ritorno in Canada,
avete avuto l'opportunità di accet-
tarmi come io ero—sapendo bene
quel che stavo passando—sapendo
bene il dolore della solitudine...
della disperazione. Invece di accet-
tare quel che io facevo della mia
vita, invece di augurarmi pace e
serenità, invece di incoraggiarmi...
voi avete criticato, disprezzato e
rifiutato ... come se fossi ancora un
bambino dj sei-sette anni!*

*E poi, mi chiedete perchè io ho
avuto il muso !?*

*E voi ... perchè avevate voi il
muso? O mi sbaglio? Eravate mica
contenti voi?*

*Dal 16 Dicembre al 3 Gennaio
due settimane e mezzo per me come
pure per voi, è stata un'eternità. Se
uno sapeva quel che doveva essere,
era sì meglio che ognuno si stasse
dov'era! Quel tempo è pure passato,
ed ecco ancora una volta che voi
date la colpa a me.*

What I do remember is to
always have been indebted to
you both ... an indebtedness
to exchange my happiness for
your sacrifices.

There are several examples—from
when I was small (do you
remember the famous bicycle that
was mine and not mine?) to a few
weeks ago (with your renuncia-
tion of Darlene).

During this last occasion, that is
your return visit to Canada, you
had the opportunity to accept me
as I was—knowing very well what
I was going through—knowing
well the pain of loneliness... of
desperation. Instead of accept-
ing what I was experiencing in
my life, instead of wishing me
happiness and serenity, instead of
encouraging me ... you have criticized, despised, and renounced...
as if I was still a child six-seven
years old!

And then you ask me why I was
upset. Am I wrong? Were you
happy for me?

From December 16 to January
3 ... two-and-a-half weeks ... for
me as for you, were an eternity. If
one had known what was to be,
yes, it would have been best for
everyone to stay where they were!
That opportunity is past us, and
yet, one more time, you assign
fault to me.

* * *

*La vostra lettera continua
a offendermi.*

*Mi offendete quando v'intromettete
tra me e mio figlio.*

*È nella lettera, che voi avete il
coraggio di dirmi di… stare vicino
a Marco, che lui ne ha bisogno!*

Chi è che vi da quest'autorità?

*State forse cercando di comprare
gli affetti di mio figlio con i
vostri risparmi!*

*State forse cercando di sostituire
l'affetto mai datomi, con quello
che date adesso a mio figlio? Con i
vostri miseri soldi, voi continuate a
intromettervi nei fatti che—come
la penso io—sono fatti di padre
e figlio!*

*E la ragione che voi vi date per
intromettervi, è che Bruno sta
perdendo la sua ragione!*

*Questo per me, è un'altro esempio
di critica… di disprezzo… e
di sentenza!*

*Ebbene, quel che io sento e dico, e
sentirò e dirò sempre a mio figlio,
è che io gli voglio bene gli voglio
bene come un padre vuol bene a un
figlio. La porta del mio cuore e della
mia casa è, e rimarrà sempre aperta
per lui.*

* * *

Your letter continues to
offend me.

You offend me when you place
yourselves between my son and
me. It is in that letter that you
have the courage to tell me to stay
close to Marc, that he needs it!

Who is it that gives you
this authority?

Are you by chance trying to buy
the affection of my son with
your savings?

Are you trying to substitute the
affection you never gave me with
that you give my son?

With your meager savings,
you continue to intrude in the
affairs—as I think of them—
between a father and his son!

And the reason you give for your
intrusion is that… Bruno is
losing his reasoning!

This for me is yet another
example of criticism… of
contempt… and of judgment!

Well, what I feel for and say to,
and will always feel for and will
always say to my son, is that I love
him… that I love him as a father
loves a son. And that the door to
my heart and to my house are and
will always be open to him.

*Però, quel che io sto cercando
d'insegnargli è che, come nella
vita, così nella mia casa ci sono e ci
saranno sempre delle regole che lui
dovrà ubbidire e rispettare.*

*Questa è la semplice legge del mio
cuore, e della mia casa.*

*E voi, come pure la signora
di vostra figlia, in questi casi,
non c'entrate.*

*Invece di darmi sostegno (di quel
che io cerco di fare), voi invece
v'intromettete e, criticate ancora.*

*Quante volte nel passato, voi due
mi avete rimproverato per come io
crescevo mio figlio? Quante volte mi
avete detto che io lo viziavo?*

*Son sicuro che io abbia sbagliato
non solo una, ma parecchie volte. E
forse l'ho viziato.*

*Ma, son pur passati quasi ventidue
anni, e pare a me che lui, Marco,
è tutto là. E io ne son fiero
dei risultati!*

What I am attempting to teach
him, however, is that in life, as in
my household, there are and will
always be rules that he will have
to obey and respect.

This is the simple law of my heart
and of my house.

For you two, as well as for your
daughter in these affairs, there is
no room. Instead of supporting
me in my endeavor (what I am
trying to achieve), you intrude
yourselves and criticize me still.

How many times in the past have
you two reproached me for how
I was raising my son? How many
times have you told me that I was
spoiling him?

I have no doubt that I have made
mistakes … not once, but several
times. And perhaps I have spoiled
him. But twenty-two plus years
have passed, and it seems to me
that Marc is all there. And I am
proud of the result that is my son.

* * *

*Quanto a voi genitori, io offro quel
che io cerco da mio figlio—cioè,
rispetto e accettazione.*

*Io, come figlio, vi rispetto al quanto
provo possibile.*

*E vi accetto per quel che voi siete;
per quel che avete fatto della
vostra vita.*

To you, my parents, I offer what
I hope from my son—that is,
respect and acceptance.

I, as a son, respect you as much as
it is possible.

And I accept you for what you
are, for all that you have accomplished in your life.

149

Il mio rispetto sarà sempre basato sull'onestà, sulla verità, e sui miei sentimenti di cuore; e non sarà mai contro la mia coscienza!

Pare che ultimamente, voi chiedete un rispetto che abbia un senso unico.

Non è un rispetto che bilancia i miei poteri con i vostri desiderii— voi quasi quasi volete che io dia senza nessun dubbio ... e la ragione è, che voi siete i miei genitori, e che avete sacrificato tutta la vostra vita per i vostri figli.

* * *

Adesso, mi minacciate con parole che promettano azioni contro di me ... minacce legate a soldi forse (?) ... a vostri sacrifici ... a vostri egoistici desiderii.

E le scuse per queste vostre decisioni saranno ...?

che Bruno non vi rispetta che Bruno non ragiona più che Bruno si è perduto!

Come vi ripeto—so io quel che sono, e agisco sentendo il mio cuore, la mia coscienza.

Seppure, sento dolore, sento mancanza—è un dolore e una mancanza che, col tempo, passerà.

My respect will always be based on honesty, on truth, and on my heart-felt feelings, and it will never be against my conscience!

It seems to me that, as of late, you ask of me a respect that is one way and one way only. It is not a respect that balances what I have to give to your desires—you almost want that I give willingly and without doubt ... and your reasoning for this is that you are my parents, and that you have sacrificed your whole life for me.

* * *

Now you threaten me with words that promise actions against me ... threats that are perhaps tied to money (?) ... to your sacrifices ... to your egotistical wishes.

And your excuses for such actions will be ...?

... that Bruno does not respect you ... that Bruno has lost the faculty of reason ... that Bruno is lost!

As I repeat—I know who I am, and I act from my heart and my conscience.

Even if I feel pain. If I feel a void, it is a pain and a void that, with time, will pass.

*Nella lettera voi parlate di Giuda
ebbene, Giuda tradì Gesu per
pochi danari.*

*Non è che forse voi, volete com-
prarvi il mio rispetto (e quello di
mio figlio) con i vostri danari?*

*Se io accettassi questi danari,
tradirò non soltanto voi, ma me
stesso. Il mio rispetto (come spero
pure quello di mio figlio) non
ha prezzo.*

Il mio cuore è sempre aperto.

*Come l'è per mio figlio, la porta del
mio cuore è aperta anche per voi.*

*Voi minacciate che in appresso
farete come voi volete—ebbene, non
avete sempre fatto cosi?*

*Vi ho sempre detto, e vi dirò sempre
che a me i vostri soldi non servono.
Preferisco che ve li godete voi fino
all'ultimo centesimo!*

* * *

*Quanto ai vostri soldi in banca al
Canada—giorni fa, ho ricevuto
una facsimile da non so' dove (?) che
mi dirige a spostare i vostri danari
alla banca di vostra figlia.*

In your letter you speak of
Judas ... Judas betrayed Jesus for a
few coins.

Could it be perhaps that you
are trying to buy my respect
(and that of my son) with your
few coins?

If I was to accept these offerings,
I would betray not only you, but
myself also.

My respect (and I hope that of
my son as well) has no price.

My heart is always open.

As it is for my son, the door to
my heart is always open also
for you.

You threaten that in the future
you will do as you please. Have
you not always done so?

I have always told you, and will
always tell you, that I have no
need for your money.

I much prefer that you enjoy
your earnings to the last
cent yourselves!

* * *

Regarding your money held in the
Canadian bank, a few days ago, I
received a fax not sure where from
(?) directing me to transfer any
remaining funds of yours to your
daughter's bank account.

151

*Purtroppo, la vostra banca
ha bisogno di una lettera di
autorizazione da voi, per qual-
siasi cambiamento ai vostri conti,
inclusi gl'indirizzi.*

*Da parte mia, io ho tolto quel
ch'era mio dal vostro libretto, e
prossimamente, se me lo fanno
fare, mi toglierò completamente
come firmatario.*

* * *

*Vi abbraccio affettuosa-
mente, Bruno.*

I have tried to do so, but the bank
requests written authorization
from you before implementing
any changes to the account.

For my part, I have taken what
was mine from the account and,
if the bank will allow me, I will
take myself off as a signatory of
your account.

* * *

An affectionate hug, Bruno.

Main entrance of *Palazzo Gagliardi* on *Via Angelo Santilli*

CHAPTER 19

La Fuga
The Getaway

ONCE AGAIN, I'M ON ITALIAN SOIL. FEELING EXHAUSTED. THIS time, my wife is with me. For her company, I made promises. We would not be staying with *Mamma e Papà*. And we would not devote the whole twenty-one days to them. I agreed to a romantic getaway. Just the two of us. At a seaside resort.

I dread seeing my parents. How will I explain the fact that we have decided to stay at a bed and breakfast? How will I convey the notion of a romantic getaway? I am sure they will put the blame on my wife. How she controls me. Or how I allow her to manipulate me. I am weak. I cannot stand up for them who have sacrificed so much for me. I regret the decision to not have come alone. Everything would be much simpler. It is said that insanity is doing the same thing over and over again and expecting different results. I must be insane.

It is 1:00 P.M. local time. My guess is that they are resting. We'll go see them at 4:00 P.M. The bed and breakfast isn't very far. Not more than a ten-minute drive. Our room is on the ground floor. Instead of a window, we have a large double glass door leading to a shaded patio. Beyond the patio, under a bright sun, is the pool. My wife splashes in the water as I lie, fully clothed, on the bed. To rejuvenate, she has chosen swimming. I prefer darkness.

This is the second time my wife and I are in Italy together. The first time was about five years ago, shortly after we got married. Back then, I had wanted *Mamma e Papà* to meet my new wife. Naively, I believed that they had been worried about me. As if I was a child. By visiting them, I had wanted to show proof that I was no longer alone. I needed them to be happy with me. For me.

Yet how could I forget those interminable three weeks? The promise to myself to never repeat the same mistake. How could I possibly believe that they had changed? Did I actually think they had softened with age? Every day became an opportunity to chastise myself. I had been so wrong in assuming that my decision to stay with them was a rational one. Maybe it could have been for a day or two, but three weeks? My new wife, like many others before her, was not welcome in my parents' home.

As I drive, these memories rush to crowd my mind. I start to feel anxious. Breathe, Bruno, breathe, I remind myself. I come to the intersection. The cemetery, to the left, their house, to the right. I turn right and see *Mamma* standing at the edge of the terrace, both hands on the railing, waiting. I make a sharp left turn in front of the gate to their driveway. It is closed. I maneuver the car to park alongside the fence, parallel to the road. *Mamma* squints to confirm that it is indeed us. She doesn't offer a smile but a frustrated look instead. One that says, "Finally, you decided to show up. Kept us waiting all this time." *Papà* appears beside her. He waves his hand. Something is up. I can tell. They've had an argument. Probably about us.

I hear them coming down the stairs. *Papà* unlocks the front door, and *Mamma* continues her way down the last flight. We hug awkwardly. We then turn around and follow them slowly up the stone steps. *Mamma* hangs on to the balustrade and pulls herself up, one step at a time. Without speaking a word, she tells me that her legs are bad. That she is in pain. Constantly. My heart cringes. I wish I could do something to help her. *Papà* too is struggling a bit, but not as much as *Mamma*. He maintains his facade. Or tries to. They have aged since I last saw them. I am here. To help them.

And so it begins. The trap has snapped. Their prayers are answered. The four of us sit on the terrace and exchange pleasantries. About our trip. About the hotel we are staying at. About their health. About life in general. My intuition was right. They have argued. I can tell by the way they talk to us. Independently. *Papà* directs his queries to my wife, while *Mamma* communicates with me, mostly through her eyes. She conveys the same things she tells me over the phone when I call her from Canada. That she is tired. Of living. With this man who's been her captor for so many decades. Why does she continue to breathe? He doesn't lift a finger to help her. Just sits at the table like a lump of lard, expecting to be served. He is old, he says, but what about her? She's not getting any younger herself, is she? She's not as strong as she used to be. He treats her like an animal. A servant. Has no manners. Not a bone of tenderness. And on she goes. Over the ever-familiar list of grievances. She pleads her case to me as if I'm there to judge and absolve her of any blame.

After a little hesitation from us, and some insistence from them, we stay for supper. *Mamma* asks me to help her set the table, while *Papà* and my wife remain on the terrace. *Mamma* apologizes for the meager offerings, but she didn't know when to expect us. Besides, the fridge is practically empty. She's been waiting for *his* relatives—meaning my cousins on *Papà*'s side of the family—to take her shopping. She says they are always busy. She has to beg them for the quick jaunt to *EuroSpin*. If *Papà* had only learned how to drive, she says, they could have had a car and wouldn't be dependent on these *milords!* As if it was the end of the world they were taking her to! And, mind you, they don't do it for free. They're always handsomely compensated for their trouble! With her legs as they are, she can barely get across the street! But who listens to her? No one!

In the meantime, as her list of grievances grows, so does the accumulation of dishes on the kitchen table. From the fridge, she brings out cheeses, crushed olives, and leftover dishes. From one of the cupboards, she pulls out a jar of homemade sausages. She hands me a knife and a cutting board and tells me to fish the sausages out and cut them in thin slices, the way I like them. Soon the table surface is overflowing with a variety of tempting bites. She knows, of course, that I like pickled eggplant. Magically, a jar materializes in front of me. "I saved this especially for you," she says. "See if your father and your wife want to come in and eat." From behind the kitchen door, *Papà* produces a half-bottle of wine and, without asking, fills the four glasses on the table to the brim. He then exchanges the empty bottle with a full one from the same hidden corner. "*A la salute!* To health!" he says. We all pick up a glass and drink.

If there were communication barriers before, the wine now ensures a quick meltdown. After a glass or two, conversation flows freely, especially where *Mamma* is concerned. She has dislodged any encumbrance she may have felt earlier and begins to voice a number of requests. I must take her shopping. Of course, only if I have some time available, she's quick to add. This is not a one-outing affair. I know from past experience. For every product, she has a particular store in mind—usually one that has the best price. Her ultimate goal, she tells me, is to replenish household supplies so that she can defer asking my cousins for a favor for as long as possible. Ideally, until the next time I visit. *Papà* too has a request: to pick up a dozen or so gallons of wine. He says that it's much cheaper to buy it by the gallon. And this way, no one has to put their nose in his personal affairs. It's nobody's business how much he drinks! To each request I answer with a "no problem" and that we can start the process as early as tomorrow. However, I did not consider that, because *Mamma* can't walk for long periods of time, each store represents an outing, and each outing represents a day. Our three weeks begin to fill in rapidly, but shopping is not the end-all.

The next item in *Mamma's* and *Papà's* affairs deals with the trouble they're having with the couple in the apartment below. Recently, they have sought legal advice and are now considering suing. I am asked to go with them and meet with their lawyer. *Papà's* increased loss of hearing allows him to interpret one thing for another. And *Mamma*, well, what can she do with nobody to talk things over with? Can I accompany them next week? If I don't mind, that is.

On personal health, *Papà* has a doctor's appointment coming up. Again, because he doesn't hear so well, someone needs to go with him to know what the doctor says. His nephew is busy. Can I go? And then *Mamma* needs to get her right leg X-rayed. Oh, and *Papà* needs to go for a blood test before he sees the doctor.

If that wasn't enough, on yet another front, *Mamma* needs to update her identity card. Somehow, those imbeciles in the municipal office mixed up her birth date. After eighty years, they have discovered that she wasn't born on the eighth of September but the ninth instead. This requires new paperwork. Without a car, they can't get it done. Can I help? Yes, of course, I can help. And, for sure, I will. Do I have a choice?

My to-do list grows by the minute. Feeling responsible, I consent to each of their requests and forget, for the time being, the promises I made to my wife prior to coming to Italy. To help them was the purpose of my trip, was it not? Pretty soon a week has gone by, and the second is already heavily booked.

My wife has been accommodating thus far, but she's bored and feels ignored. A couple of times, she reminds me of the week-by-the-sea I promised her. Reluctantly, I negotiate the seven days down to a mere twenty-four hours. Angry and frustrated, she demands we stay at the luxurious Grand Hotel, *Le Rocce*, in the seaside town of Gaeta. The price of one night is the same as a week at a typical resort. During the drive to the coast, we examine the entrapment we feel immersed in. She expresses her resentment, while I continue to excuse *Mamma's* on-going criticisms. As the Tyrrhenian Sea opens before us, I take a deep breath and wish for us to be free of the burden that is my mother, if only for a day.

We stumble into the hotel lobby looking bedraggled. The staff greets us eagerly and directs us to our suite. There are no elevators, so we're forced to drag our suitcases up and down a series of stone steps. The view from our room is stunning. A deep-blue sky reflected in a turquoise sea. A warm breeze drifts through the balcony doors. We shed our tired clothes for hotel-supplied robes and sit on the balcony with Champagne in celebration. A sigh of relief. A while later, we put on our swimsuits and go to the pool. We settle into lounge chairs in the sun.

To energize, my wife decides to swim laps in the pool. I haven't yet found a way to relax. I sit stiffly, a bundle of nerves. I can't shake the thought of *Mamma*. I am haunted by her. Later, back in our room, we make love, slowly. No reprieve. I observe my wife's gentle breathing as she rests peacefully. A moment of envy and then a wave of anger. We ready ourselves for dinner. Our table is under a starry sky. We order. We sip. We eat. We sip some more. Silently. There is nothing to talk about if not about the situation we are so desperately trying to escape. Shadows move to the flickering of candlelight. In the obscurity, I recognize the apprehension in my wife's eyes. I am fearful. This will be too much for her to bear. She is going to leave.

I'm disheartened by the fact that I can't enjoy myself. My

mother, she is the only one to blame for our plight. Why can I not rebel? It's my fault. Yes, it's all my doing. Am I a slow learner? I must be. I drink more wine. More Champagne. I find no salvation.

The following morning, I am dead tired. Check-out is at 2:00 P.M.. We have a few hours left in this paradise. Perhaps there's still time for me to recoup. Two recliners await us in the small cove. The surrounding cliffs create a barrier to the rest of the world. I feel claustrophobic. I see the water, but the larger Mediterranean is far beyond my field of vision. A cloudless sky with a radiant sun. My wife asks me to rub suntan lotion into her skin. I close my eyes and hear children splashing about in the water. I open them and see waves reach the shore and the rugged rocks that jut out along the white sand.

Across the water on the opposite shore, I see the many other hotels we could have stayed at. All far less expensive. I hear my mother's voice in my head say, "You like to throw money away, don't you? It means you didn't sweat for it, that's what it means." I want to scream. My body quivers with a surge of guilt. I feel a tug from the anchor of the ever-present infernal vortex.

❃

2016 - Grand Hotel, *Le Rocce*, Gaeta, Italy

2016 – View of *Sant'Elia Fiumerapido* from *Mamma e Papà*'s front yard

CHAPTER 20

Piccolo Uomo Grande
Little Big Man

IT IS LATE AFTERNOON, MID-AUTUMN. *PAPÀ* SITS SILENT, WEDGED in the corner at the end of the hallway. He stares blankly at the horizon through the glass door to the terrace. Diagonally across, I observe him as if through a set of binoculars. A faint draft threads through puffs of white hair. Aided by his rhythmic breathing, it fills the folds of skin over his desolate face. Rebellious whiskers flaunt their recent escape from the razor's edge, while unspoken words remain frozen on retreating lips. The light from his grey-green eyes slowly fades. I take a deep breath. Bittersweet sorrow fills my lungs.

Papà is ninety years old. He's the youngest of six brothers: *Alfredo, Giovanni, Antonio, Mario,* and *Alessandro*. Not one of them lived past sixty. Aware of his longevity, he credits his brothers for his long life. "I'm living the years left behind by my brothers. May they rest in peace." His brothers may have left him time, but they didn't leave him any room for gratification. In the end, *Papà* fails to fulfill his life-long ambition to attain status within the brotherhood circle. By dying when they did, his older siblings have denied him any chance at being recognized for his achievements. *Papà* remains the runt of the family. Circumstances may have prevented *Papà* from attending his brothers' funerals. And now, as if out of spite, his brothers will not attend his burial. He will die alone and wanting.

I sympathize with *Papà*'s longing. Like him, I too have hungered for recognition. For as long as I can remember, *Papà* has consistently ignored my accomplishments, as well as my attempts to connect with him on an equal footing.

Now the man across from me drifts away. He is no longer accessible. What I see is a man alone, gasping for air, as the noose around his neck tightens. I have no other choice than to accept that our time has run out.

"I'll be fine. I have done enough emotional work to accept this," I reassure myself. Still, something is pulling me down towards a void of darkness.

I don't consider *Papà* a big man. Or a significant man. Never have. During my childhood, I couldn't help but see him in contrast to his brothers. The stance of my uncles overshadowed any of *Papà*'s efforts at projecting authority. His brothers oozed power and strength. My cousins, for example, boasted of their fathers' war adventures: *Zio Mario* had been a prisoner behind the Russian line; *Zio Alfredo* had fought in Africa; and *Zio Giovanni* had been a member of the elite Italian *Bersaglieri* army core.

I don't blame *Papà* for his lack of military accomplishments, for I understand that he had been too young to be a recruit. But I don't give him credit for surviving that treacherous period, or for having lost his mother to the war. Or for taking on the important, but not so glamorous, task of cooking and cleaning for his brethren. Getting married was *Papà's* first attempt at individuation. He had to show his brothers that he could take care of a family. Even though *Papà* ran *Zio Mario's* tailor shop almost single-handedly, his compensation was, as *Mamma* would say, "… a mere pittance, barely enough to feed a family of three!"

Mamma's endless bellyaching about how she cannot make ends meet pushes *Papà* to action. Because he can't stand up to his brother and ask for more money, he seeks opportunities to get out of Italy. He applies to immigrate to Australia, the United States of America, Switzerland, and France. France is the first to offer him a chance. He accepts and joins a construction crew. He goes from delicate tailoring to bricklaying, sleeps in rat-infested barracks, and eats canned foods. Sadly, he can't endure it. A month later, he's back in his hometown, totally emaciated and beaten. Humbled, he asks *Zio Mario* for his job back. His brother concedes, but not without dishing out a good dose of scorn. Soon *Papà* is back at the helm, underpaid, and running his brother's shop.

Years pass. A fourth mouth is added to the struggling family, that of my sister. Not much changes with respect to *Papà's* income. *Mamma's* whining and crying continues non-stop to the point of wearing down *Papà's* patience. Exasperated, he decides to once again look outside Italy for a solution. This time, he answers Canada's call for tradespeople. The response is positive. He passes their criteria for immigration, and soon he's packing to leave. Of course, his brothers think they have seen this all before. They won't give him credit. In fact, they sneer at his brave little act and openly predict another disgraceful return within a year of his departure. Assuming, of course, that he has money for the return fare. Their negativity, however, does not deter *Papà*. In fact, it serves to strengthen his resolve. He is going to show them, just you wait and see!

Papà is in his mid-thirties when, alone, he boards the Italian ocean liner *La Vulcania* for the unknown Canada. He leaves his young family behind and courageously forges a fresh start, going on to disprove every last malicious omen his brothers had predicted. After spending as many years in Canada as he had in Italy, in his early seventies, *Papà* returns to his native land, a proud man, but his brothers are all dead and buried.

Notwithstanding all his achievements, *Papà* remains a little big man. For one, he tried way too hard to impress his brothers. For another, he gave them power to manipulate him. He was reactive rather than proactive or strategic. And for yet another, he forever sought approval from them. Deep down, he wanted to be treated as an equal, a true member of the tribe. But all to no avail. Perhaps it was because his brothers were envious of the tangibles their little brother showed, such as owning his own house and having a son who had completed university to become an engineer. Or perhaps it was because his brothers were ignorant of all the hard work the little brother had been capable of. The fact remains that they simply ignored *Papà*. With time, that lack of recognition festered seeds of resentment that turned *Papà* into the bitter old man I see sitting across from me today.

A river of discontent has been flowing under *Papà*'s skin for a long time. Growing up, I often experienced its threatening force. In a flash, his joviality could burst into a blasphemous and frightening roar.

I close my eyes. I hear his barks. The terrifying sound of plates and glasses shattering on the kitchen floor, into the fireplace. I cringe. *Mamma* is crying. He is shouting. Swearing. Cursing. Like a mudslide, insults flow without resistance. I am afraid to open my eyes.

The clashes between husband and wife take place mostly on Monday nights, when *Papà* worked a half-day. In the afternoon, he doesn't come home for lunch. Instead, he meets up with a couple of his friends and brothers for a game of *Bocce*. It's not just one game, but two, maybe three. And a winner's reward has to be a bottle of beer, or two. By evening, the buoyant group migrates from playing *Bocce* and drinking beer outdoors, to playing cards and drinking wine indoors.

Some Mondays, I'm lucky enough to tag along with *Papà*. I say lucky because when *Zio Alfredo* is part of the group, during a card game, he gives me money to go to *Giovannino's* shop and buy *mezzo-chilo di pagnotta e cinquanta grammi di provolone—provolone piccante, non dolce* (half a kilo of bread and fifty grams of provolone cheese—strong, not mild). My reward is the leftover change, a share of the ten-to-one ratio of bread and cheese, and a glass of watered-down wine.

The cantina where the group plays *Scopa* and drinks wine is called *Alberto Panzone*. It's not very far from where we live. On these Monday nights, however, the five-minute walk turns into an hour-long journey. The three or four drunken brothers stagger along the narrow pathway discussing the precarious state of the universe. Their deep voices bounce off the stone tunnel, alerting everyone to the impending crisis. They stop here and there to emphasize a point. Tired and sleepy, I stay close to *Papà's* side, feeling the effect of the glass of wine. Finally, when we reach the portal of *Palazzo Gagliardi*, I tug *Papà's* coat tail to ask if I can go upstairs.

"Go. And tell your mother I'll be up in a minute," he slurs.

Liberated, I run up the three flights of stairs. The door to the apartment isn't locked. *Mamma* is sitting at the table, waiting. I can tell she's been crying. Her eyes are red, the sockets dark and recessed, and her cheeks wet. The table is set for one, for *Papà*. She turns her bloodshot eyes in my direction and begins to berate me for ruining dinner. I know it's not my fault, but I don't say anything because I don't want to add to her sorrow. I let her practice on me what she's going to say to *Papà*. When she's complete, she orders me to bed. I cowardly obey and disappear into the dark bedroom, leaving the door ajar. Soundlessly, I change into my pajamas and slip between the sheets on my cot at the far corner of the room. And wait.

I hear *Papà*'s whistle as he comes up the stairs. The whistling becomes louder as he approaches. The door opens. The whistling stops. Then chaos. I pull my blanket tight around my head, but to no avail.

The uproar finally subsides. All that remains is *Mamma*'s monotonous sobbing. If at first I take *Papà*'s side, now I am with *Mamma*. I don't want her to cry anymore. *Papà* was too loud. Too rough with her. I got scared. I wish I could have stopped him. Protect *Mamma*. But I was paralyzed by his roars.

The door slams open. I keep my eyes shut because I don't want them to know that I'm awake. *Papà* enters the bedroom. Clumsily, he undresses and flops onto the bed. Within seconds, his snores fill the room. *Mamma* is in the kitchen cleaning up the mess. When she's done, she turns off the light and comes to the bedroom. In the darkness, I follow her movements by the sound of her whimpering as she slips beside her husband. Riding the endless wave of snivels, I surrender to a restless sleep. I dream I am a Roman soldier. I stand guard outside *Mamma*'s tent.

Papà and his brothers
From left to right: 1960s - *Zio Mario, Zio Antonio, Zio Alfredo*
… 1970s - *Zio Giovanni, Zio Alessandro* e *Papà*

Papà with his oldest nephew
… like the 'good old
days'… almost.

2013 - Cousin *Elio (Zio
Antonio's son) e Papà* on *Via
Angelo Santilli*

CHAPTER 21

Fiducia
Trust

I BURIED *PAPÀ* TODAY. OR WAS IT YESTERDAY? OR WILL IT BE tomorrow? I'm not sure anymore. It's all so confusing. And I'm so tired. It depends on the time zone I place myself in, I guess. According to records, he died on Sunday, May 12, 2019 at 7:00 A.M., GMT+2 (that is, *Sant'Elia Fiumerapido* time). Where I live, it would be 10:00 P.M., PST, the day before, or Saturday, May 11.

I say buried, but, in actuality, *Papà* is "shelved." His coffin is cemented on a shelf in a wall of the new addition to the cemetery. A few years ago, he and *Mamma* bought slots numbered "53" and "54." They chose the type, size, and location of their final resting place. The only decision left to me was the individual placement. Top or bottom. I decided to place *Papà* at ground level, in number 53, and *Mamma* on the shelf above, number 54.

I've been in Italy for four exhausting weeks already. My return flight home remains open. I am overwhelmed by the number of items I have to address before I can leave. Most importantly, I'm waiting to see how *Mamma* copes with *Papà's* passing and with her new living arrangements. I'm unsure how long I can endure this stress, however. I wasn't ready for this trip. It seems to me I was here not long ago.

In fact, it's been less than eight months since I dropped in to see how *Mamma e Papà* were doing with their new setup. Against my recommendation, *Papà* had decided to hire a live-in caregiver and to keep *Mamma* at home with him, even though her paralysis persisted and his health continued to slide. The reception I received the few times I visited was extremely awkward. It felt as if I was visiting strangers. *Mamma e Papà* behaved like school children under heavy supervision. Their babysitter, a sturdy woman from Albania who spoke broken Italian, had taken control of their household. She gave me a tour of the apartment. The guest bedroom was now her room. My parent's bedroom was rearranged to incorporate a hospital bed for *Mamma* and a piece of machinery used to lift her in and out of the bed to her wheelchair. Their old queen-size bed was squished to one side of the room, leaving just enough of a walkway for *Papà* to use. The dining/living room was also rearranged to accommodate other medical devices that were used for *Mamma's* care. It was no longer the pristine living quarters of before.

Typically, the four of us sat in the hallway, just outside the kitchen, where the air felt thick and heavy, like a weighted blanket. Conversation was stymied and superficial. Because of her stroke, *Mamma* couldn't talk. But she repeatedly aimed her downward gaze toward me to convey her miserable state. Aware, I tried hard to ignore the lure. There was nothing I could do for her. She had followed her husband's lead. *Papà*, on the other hand, appeared embarrassed by my unexpected appearance on the scene, as if caught in some mischievous act. He didn't have much to say to me except that, "the two of us are managing okay. In our own house and not in some institution surrounded by *crazy* people." None of the visits afforded me an opportunity to dig deeper and gather more insight. The best I could achieve was to establish a connection with their nurse. I told her that I was the one she should notify in the event of an emergency. Night or day, anytime.

In contrast, my current visit was instigated by the man himself. As far as I can recall, it was the one and only time *Papà* has requested my presence. Somehow, he must have sensed that his time was nearly up. That he had to relinquish and entrust me with the control of his affairs. Reluctantly, I suspect. Because he made sure that the messenger relayed to me that, "the costs will be covered by your father." This is typical behavior. He pays; therefore, he is absolved of any wrong outcome. The only difference now, of course, is that he no longer knows what he's doing. His actions are strictly visceral.

I can't recall a time when *Papà* willingly placed trust in me, not even partially. I don't know why. I've never asked him directly. Perhaps it was out of some sort of male competition. A need to feel superior, even at the expense of his own son. Did he not grow up in the shadow of his six older brothers? Had he not lived a life of inferiority? He had no other knowledge but to raise me under his shadow. To keep me in constant fear of his wrath, even if it was hollow. That's why, I suppose, he never applauded my successes. He never accepted my suggestions, even though I went to great lengths to prove to him that they were well-founded. And he never gave me an opportunity where my opinion counted. This last chapter of his life—from *Mamma's* stroke to his demise—is a prime example of what our relationship has been like. He was the almighty father, and I the ever-obedient son.

When I arrived four weeks ago, it was total chaos. *Papà* was in hospital. Status undetermined. *Mamma* was at home. When I met with her caregiver, she presented me with a list of things that were lacking. The fridge required restocking. There were prescriptions to be filled. Bills to be paid. Appointments to be kept. Others to be made. And she needed a break. *Mamma*'s cousin's daughter, who substituted for her two hours in the afternoon every day, was busy with personal matters. She also told me to get in touch with *Papà*'s nephew if I wanted more information.

Mamma's cousin's daughter and *Papà*'s nephew are the two individuals who have facilitated my parents' current setup and are intimately familiar with their current state of affairs. Both were unavailable for an immediate briefing, so I had no choice but to act. And act fast. Between visits to the hospital to see *Papà* and visits to the house to see *Mamma*, I reestablished connection with my prior contacts and began to take the necessary steps. I searched and secured space in a care home at the edge of town. Signed contracts for both *Mamma e Papà* to move in as soon as possible. Terminated the services of the in-home nurse. Began the process of decluttering my parents' apartment to ready it for sale. And sought legal advice to take total control of my parents' affairs.

On Wednesday, April 24, ten days after my arrival, *Papà* was transported by ambulance from *Ospedale Santa Scolastica*, where he'd spent the past several days undergoing tests and analyses, to *Villa San Francesco*, the home for elder care I'd contracted with. The next day, April 25, *Mamma* was moved from the apartment that they had occupied since their move back to Italy in 2001, also to *Villa San Francesco* to be with her husband.

Neither parent, *Papà* nor *Mamma*, was ecstatic about the move. *Mamma* couldn't speak, so her sentiments were a little difficult to gauge, but she was not pleased. And *Papà*, although increasingly oblivious to his surroundings, thought the move to be a temporary one and that soon I'd be taking him back to his home. Unfortunately for him, his health continued on a downward spiral and on May 12 he passed on.

Papà did not die peacefully. He left this world unsettled. And if he was still around to point a finger, he would point it at me. My fault for not executing his instructions to a T. No one else's. Whatever decision I took went against the grain. Against his will. Had he had it his way, he would have preferred his nephew, or the daughter of *Mamma*'s cousin, to act on his behalf. At least they listened to him.

With the latter I had a good rapport, but it ended a few months before *Papà*'s death. With the former, I never had much of a connection. It seemed to me that whenever I was present, he would minimize his involvement with my parents. In the past two decades, this nephew has been in and out of *Papà*'s favor. When in favor, *Papà* relied on him to lend a hand here and there. Sometimes with the garden. Sometimes with an errand to run. And sometimes with a house repair. These services were always well compensated. Sometimes over-compensated.

With *Mamma*'s cousin's daughter, I freely shared the dilemma I faced the time I rushed to Italy to deal with *Mamma*'s cerebral stroke. She and I discussed the possibility of putting both *Mamma e Papà* in a care home. On principle we disagreed, but in the end, she conceded that it was my choice. Notwithstanding my decision, when I left, she sided with *Papà* and helped him keep *Mamma* at home and hire a *badante*, a live-in caregiver, to look after *Mamma* primarily, as well as cook and clean for them both.

Mamma e Papà don't trust easily. In fact, I don't know if they've ever truly trusted anyone, including one another. They are suspicious by nature and always on alert, especially when it comes to money. Their whole life they have worked hard. Saved zealously. Spent guardedly. And avoided debt as much as possible. Unfortunately for *Papà*, at the end of his life, he left this world with an unresolved financial situation dear to his heart.

Shortly after my arrival, he confided in me about a bundle of cash he'd been accumulating. He told me that he was saving to cover some of the cost for resurfacing the pavement on the terrace. He further explained that every time he went to the bank, he withdrew a few hundred euros from the accounts and added them to the stash. He kept this money hidden and locked in the armoire in his bedroom. The exact figure he did not quite remember—around 3,500 EUR. And he couldn't pinpoint the exact location either—in a coat pocket, in an envelope buried under some blanket, or in a box in a bottom corner of the cabinet. To put his mind at ease, I searched for this bundle from one end of the armoire to the other, and from one coat pocket to the next. I found no treasure. I reported my unsuccessful searches to him. And each time, he got very agitated. He would regurgitate the same set of clues and instructions, assuring me that the money had to be there. I just hadn't looked thoroughly enough. Finally, when he began to accept the fact that perhaps the money was indeed not there, he started to explore other possibilities. Who could have taken it? There were only two viable choices: the caregiver or his nephew. He directed me to ask them. I did so via text. The replies were both ambiguous. I let it go. And *Papà* passed on.

Now that he's dead, I'm left with the onerous task of sorting through the mess he left behind. I don't much mind the cleaning-up aspect, but I do mind the resentment seething in me, and the fact that I am alone. For the time being, *Mamma* remains in purgatory. She's suspended in her own infantile world. My self-imposed sense of duty is to ensure that she will be adequately looked after. Sure, I could leave her be, but I cannot. Period. My sister says, "What can I do from so far away?" Nothing, of course. She is excused. But why can't I use her excuse? I have no answer. All I can say is that I cannot ignore *Mamma*.

The list of things to address is overwhelming. In my mind, I weigh the pros and cons of each action item. The apartment remains cluttered and unkempt. Why not simply give it away? To charity? But how? And did *Mamma e Papà* not work hard for it? Would they be happy? Bank accounts remain blocked and inaccessible. I should just forget them. Why not? But why? Didn't *Mamma e Papà* sweat blood to earn every penny? Invoices keep surfacing and mounting. Why don't I change my name and simply vanish as the heir? But *Mamma e Papà* would have wanted the bills to be paid without delay. It's their reputation I would be destroying. Back and forth I go as I continue to justify moving forward, sluggishly carrying their load along with mine. The sooner I complete these tasks, I tell myself, the sooner I can go back home. Or so I imagine.

A few people accompanied the hearse to the cemetery. They have dispersed. I remain alone, by choice. I observe the mason sealing *Papà*'s coffin behind an inner layer of brick before the engraved stone covers the shelf. My mind drifts. A light wind blows. *Papà* is gone. Forever. And so is any opportunity for me to gain his approval. I have tried. Repeatedly. And I have failed. Perhaps he was right to never place trust in me. I remember a time in the distant past when I was an altar boy and walked in procession to this same cemetery to bury one of *Don Mario*'s parishioners. I noticed that the bigger the gathering, the higher the status of the deceased. In comparison, *Papà* didn't hold much status. And then, while *Don Mario* performed his ceremony, I wondered what it would feel like to be in the coffin while it was being interred, imagining somehow that the person therein was awake. I wonder if *Papà* is awake, and if he is able to hear my thoughts.

Papà has left a hole in my heart. A cauldron. A volcano that spews rage instead of lava. Killing every living organism in its path. Aborting any hope for atonement, any chance at receiving that elusive pat on the shoulder. At hearing *Papà's* voice say, "Good work, Bruno. You're a good son. I am proud of you. Thank you so much!" Anger engulfs my veins. I want to explode. A roar so loud to shake all of humanity. I want to start anew. I want *Mamma* freed from her misery, and *Papà* released from his inferiority. And I want to breathe life into my lungs. Surely there is salvation for people like us. What is our purpose otherwise?

Mamma e Papà.

CHAPTER 22
Figlio di Mamma
Mama's Boy

WEDNESDAY, JANUARY 22, 2020. *MAMMA* DIED TODAY.

My phone rings.

Caller: *Casa San Francesco.*

Time: 2:22 A.M.

I press the green button and, clearing my throat, manage a groggy, "*Pronto*." I recognize the voice at the other end. The head nurse.

"Bruno, I have some sad news… *Elena* passed a little while ago. I'm so sorry."

A half-hour later, I'm at *Mamma*'s bedside. She lies there, eyes closed. Her facial expression is, for once, completely relaxed. No sign of suffering. I touch her cheek with the back of my hand. It is cold. And dry.

"*Mamma*, where are you?" I scream in silence.

On the spur of the moment, I decide to go to Italy in mid-January. This, of course, is the worst time of the year to travel there, but I can find no other solution. I must see her.

Eight months ago, after burying *Papà*, I left *Mamma* at the care home. She was crying. Since then, I've received a few sporadic reports about her wellbeing. Rather than pacify me, the unreliable communication has intensified my worry. The guilt of knowing she is alone in a strange place consumes me.

December has always been a difficult month for me. The one just past is no exception. It's the time of the year when I become morose. This state of mind intensifies as the holiday season approaches. During this period, I add bricks to the walls of my prison. In the new year, when festivities slowly dissipate and winter sets in, I find myself entrapped in a cell. This irksome phase is traceable to my teenage years when I was starting to rebel against my parents. Instead, I chose to take on *Mamma*'s trauma, hoping to lighten her burden.

Unintentionally perhaps, *Mamma* imposes her life upon mine. Guided by anger and frustration, she makes me feel guilty for enjoying life by juxtaposing it against her tragic past. Her needs deflate my enthusiasm. She criticizes any progress that I make. Guided by shame, I practice obedience, restraint, and perseverance. Over time, I shortchange myself. Instead of love, I experience commitment. Instead of abandonment, I embrace responsibility. Instead of freedom, I seek control. I devote myself to carrying the guilt unquestioned.

After more than thirty hours of travel, I arrive at the *Cassino* exit off the A45, *Autostrada del Sole,* from Rome. Ten minutes later, at 4:25 P.M., I press the horn of my rental car to request the opening of the gate to *Casa San Francesco.* This is where *Mamma* has resided the past nine months. I couldn't have timed my arrival any better, as afternoon visiting hours at *Casa San Francesco* are from 4:30 to 6:00 P.M.

The nurse is as unfamiliar to me as I am to her. I tell her who I have come to visit, and she asks me if I'm the son from Canada, *il figlio canadese.* I nod to confirm, and with a wide, welcoming smile she leads me to the main room, where the residents are assembled for the afternoon reception. She points to *Mamma* in a wheelchair, alone in the far corner. Her head is tilted to the left and her gaze toward the floor.

"It looks like *Elena* is taking a nap."

On tiptoes, I approach *Mamma.* Gently, I place my left hand on her right shoulder.

"*Mamma,*" I whisper.

Her head snaps upright, and her eyes open wide. A wave of fear envelops me as old familiar feelings of culpability arise. She squints and, for a moment or two, doesn't recognize me. When she does, it's as if a switch turns on inside her. Instantly, her angst morphs into delight, and her lameness into elation. Her eyes shine brightly. She raises her good left hand and grabs mine still resting on her shoulder, squeezing it firmly. Her eyes lock with mine to say, "You remembered me. Finally!"

She has lost weight. Her cheekbones jut, making her eye sockets deeper and darker. My presence makes her happy. A pang of guilt pulls from the pit of my stomach. We make small talk. The room begins to fill, as does the background chatter. I am *Mamma's* only visitor. I ask if anyone from the town comes to see her. She shakes her head to say no. I take her skeletal hands in mine and assure her that I am here now. I will keep her company. The familiar light in her eyes shines as she nods agreement. She is like a child. The room is full. The chatter high. In vain, *Mamma* and I try to communicate. Her words don't come, and my interpretations don't match. Frustrated by our failed attempts, we sit in silence and hold hands. She closes her eyes and drifts off. I study her further. I recognize traces of her, but her appearance seems lifeless. *Mamma's* eyes open momentarily. I realize then that they are my only means of connection to her.

My attention shifts to the room. I observe the other patients. Listen to their visitors. Assess the nurses. The atmosphere in the room is like that of an open-air market. Chaotic. People yelling over one another. Obscenities. Slander. Curses.

"Mamma, ti trattano bene qui?" (*Mamma*, do they treat you well here?) I ask her when she awakens. I want to know how she manages this bedlam. She shakes her head. Okay? Not okay? I rephrase my question. This time she nods. I am more confused.

"Mamma, ti piacerebbe ritornare in Canada?" (*Mamma*, how would you like to come back to Canada?) Her eyes light up. Her hand grabs mine. A firm squeeze. She nods her head vigorously.

It's 6:00 P.M. Time for all visitors to leave. I put on my coat and bend down to kiss *Mamma* on the forehead. She raises her hand to my face in a gentle caress. Her tearful eyes search mine. When they lock, her gaze burns through my pupils.

"Figlio mio. Take pity on me! Save me!"

In a delirium, I toss and turn in my hotel bed, unable to let go. My body is exhausted, and my mind is agitated. *Mamma's* cry for salvation echoes inside me. The plan to free *Mamma* from the care home swirls in my mind. I must take her with me when I leave! She will not die alone. She has suffered enough. She deserves better! We are her only family. There is no one else. As her son, it is my duty. To succeed, I'll need help from my sister and my wife. They said they would help me. I told them what needs to be done. I don't want to stay here any longer, but if needed, I will stay. I'll stay with her to the end! She wants to come back to Canada. I know it. I won't leave if it's not with her. Finally, I will make her happy!

I awake to searing lower back spasms. Each movement of my body pushes a blade that opens furrows of pain. This morning, the discomfort is decisively sharper. I become aware of the thin mattress under me. The long plane trip is making itself known. I am exhausted. As I collect my thoughts, I feel anger descending upon me like a lead blanket.

How I hate to be back in this godforsaken town! Yet I am back. I curse the day *Papà* chose to return here to die. I pity myself for all I'm going through because of his decision. *Mamma* seems in a dreadful state, and the pity shifts from me to her. Why is she still alive? I recall yesterday's visit to *Casa San Francesco*. The promise to take *Mamma* back to Canada is my way of coping with my guilt. I envy the way that my sister skirts her responsibility to *Mamma*. By bringing *Mamma* to Canada, maybe the weight will shift from me to her.

No wonder getting out of bed lately is an arduous procedure. This morning is no different, except for the increased intensity of pain. I take a deep breath and begin to angle my body so that my knees are in line with the edge of the mattress. The narrow single bed limits my movement when my head reaches the opposite wall. I drop my legs to the floor and simultaneously use my arms to push up my upper body to reach a sitting position. A long exhale. Without moving my torso, I extend my right arm and press my phone on the bedside table. It lights up. The time:

7:23 A.M. I calculate the hour back home; it's yesterday, 10:23 P.M., my regular bedtime. A deep inhale as I focus on step two: standing. I plant my feet firmly on the cold cement floor and angle my upper body in such a way as to form an upside-down letter "V." Exhale. A couple of breaths to stabilize before the next move, the most painful. To spring the V open and stand up straight. As I open up, each vertebra aligns with the verte-bra next to it until my posture is straight. The pain subsides. A little relief. I then walk towards the thin vertical line of light across the room. I trip on the open suitcase lying on the floor but maintain my balance. I grab the edges and whisk the curtain panels wide open. Daylight rushes in to fill and define the room. It's small, even by European hotel standards. With the single bed and a night table on one side, and the desk with a chair and the armoire on the other, there's little free space left. No wonder I tripped! I turn to go to the bathroom. It's a compact four-piece: sink, toilet, shower, and bidet. I assess the shower stall and ques-tion if I'll be able to shower properly. I will not.

"Why the fuck am I here?" I shout.

I sip a *cappuccino* in the hotel lobby. My body feels like the after-math of a tornado. What happened yesterday? I retrace the steps from my arrival at *Casa San Francesco. Mamma* is not happy. She has never been happy, but that never stops me from making her happy. There's no one here to check on her. No other family member. Other residents have local relatives that visit them. They bring food. They ensure personal items are used accord-ingly. Yesterday, *Mamma* had some old rag over her legs to keep her warm. It wasn't hers. Where is all the stuff we brought for her? Brand-new throws? Hardly worn sweaters? Socks? I make a mental note to ask the nurse this morning.

Yes, it would be nice if she came with me when I leave in a

couple of weeks. But how? How do I move her from the care home to the airport? Within the airport? From plane to plane? And what if she needs a diaper change? For the sake of argument, let's assume that she and I make it to Canada. What about immigration? Let's further assume that we sail through. Then what? Where does she go? To live with my sister in Ontario? To live with me in British Columbia? Or do we put her in a home? My sister says she doesn't mind taking care of *Mamma* at her house. But does she realize what she's taking on? As for me, my wife and I would have to buy a larger house. A move we cannot afford. And if we put her in a home, will it be any different than where she is now? She'll be in a strange place, with strange people, and with caregivers who speak only English!

The more I think about the plan, the more unattainable it becomes. Bringing *Mamma* to Canada at this stage in her life isn't possible. And it would not make her happy.

Morning visiting hours are 10:30 to 11:45 A.M. On my way there, I stop at a nearby grocery store and pick up some snacks for *Mamma*. At 10:30 A.M., I'm back by her side. She's happy to see me. Definitely in better spirits than yesterday. Her eyes sparkle with joy as if to shout, "My son is here for me!" She enjoys the yogurt and pastries I brought for her. Like a baby, she opens her mouth to each plastic spoonful I bring to her lips. I must bring more food this afternoon, I note.

We spend the time together much like we did yesterday afternoon. Communication between us is sporadic. I ask simple questions with yes or no answers to assess her emotional state. When I ask her if she would like to come back to Canada, her response is the same as yesterday. Her eyes light up. Her hand grabs mine. A firm squeeze. And she nods her head vigorously. I lie when I tell her that I'm working on it.

My activities are arranged around the morning and afternoon visiting hours at *Casa San Francesco*. During my first week, I meet with *l'agente immobiliare* (the realtor) for a progress report on the sale of the house: some interest, but nothing serious. On more than one occasion, I meet with *il direttore di banca* (the bank manager) to consolidate and control my parents' savings. Each time he defines a new requirement: a certificate, a signature, a wrong entry to redo, and so on. I meet with *la commercialista* (the accountant) to determine municipal invoices and government taxes to be paid. I meet with *l'avvocato* (the lawyer) charged with the application for *l'amministratore di sostegno* (the support administrator), the judge-assigned trustee who will act on *Mamma*'s behalf. I meet with *il geometra* (the surveyor) to ask for a correction in *la successione* document, requested by *il direttore di banca* (the bank director). I drop in to see *la parrucchiera* (the hairdresser) to schedule an appointment to do *Mamma*'s hair and settle the charges for past monthly visits to *Casa San Francesco*. I go to the local medical offices to meet with *il dottore di famiglia* (the family doctor) to certify that *Mamma* has a disability. Finally, I meet with the newly assigned *amministratore di sostegno* (support administrator) to review *Mamma*'s file and arrive at a common agenda.

Two weeks have passed. My routine is well established. Dutifully, I continue to visit *Mamma* as much as it's allowed. We have entered a monotonous phase. Our time together has lost its vitality. For the past three days, *Mamma* has refused to engage with me. She rejects conversation, food, and company. When I arrive, I find her in her usual place, pretending to be asleep. She stubbornly holds that stance for the duration of my visit. The nurses tell me that she is fine prior to my arrival and fine after

I leave. I recognize the familiar pattern that chains us together.

Secretly, I count the hours until my flight home, but I dread the thought of returning to bury her. I abort the plan to free *Mamma* from the care home. I conceal from her that she will not be coming to Canada. She figures it out. That's why she's angry. That's why she's punishing me. There can be no secrets between *Mamma* and me. She and I share a unique fate. *Mamma* is the judge and the jury. She finds me guilty, and she labels herself as the victim. She passes sentences on the two of us. She unwillingly accepts her sentence, and I obediently accept mine.

It has taken more than six months to open the file to assign a trustee to act on *Mamma*'s behalf in all matters pertaining to her welfare. Two days after I make the introduction between *Mamma* and her trustee-designate, *Mamma* dies. As a result, the file that took months to open is back on the judge's desk, this time awaiting dissolution.

The so-called bond that binds me to *Mamma* tightens around my back and pulls me deeper into the abyss. I have swallowed a fish hook, and it remains lodged in my throat. As I gulp, it digs deeper in the sensitive tissue. I am addicted to this intensifying, sweet pain.

Unfinished business stirs the calm. The house remains on the market. The bank accounts continue to be inaccessible. And unpaid invoices accrue. A global pandemic ensues, promising to lengthen the torment.

Papà passed away last May. I have yet to mourn him. Worrying about *Mamma* has taken precedence. She has joined him now.

Mourning for her will be postponed also. Before I can bemoan the losses, I must complete their unfinished business. Tomorrow, I will place *Mamma*'s remains on top of *Papà*'s. They will be together once again. This final step was requested by them, to the last detail, years ago.

For *Mamma*'s funeral, I have chosen a simpler service. When *Papà* died, I followed the advice of the funeral director: a full-on funeral with a complete mass in the church in the center of town and townsfolk with nothing better to do than gawk in attendance. I decided to forgo the surreal theatrics for a simple blessing at the *Casa San Francesco*, *Mamma*'s last place of residence. Supporting me will be a handful of chosen friends. After the event, I'll turn my back to the town and drive to Rome, where I'll spend my last night in Italy. I look forward to the day after tomorrow, when I board the plane back home.

Mamma is gone. I feel some reprieve, but a phantom weight remains. *Mamma* does not rest. She continues to suffer. In me. Mea culpa.

May 2019 - *Mamma e Bruno*

POSTSCRIPT

A Psychotherapeutic Perspective
By Peter DeRoche, MD,
Psychiatrist, Assistant Professor
at the University of Toronto

In his memoir, *Mea Culpa: A Plea of Innocence*, Bruno Cocorocchio embarks on an archeological endeavor, a series of excavations. The site is his life. Within each chapter, or 'dig', Bruno exposes events from the past that have contributed to his damaged sense of self. Meticulously, he brings to the surface 'artifacts of life' that are the clues to his suffering. Reassembling this history enables him to understand what happened instead of who to blame for his maladjustments.

Courageously, Bruno focuses on his relationship with his parents, particularly his mother. He describes the impact of poverty and the postwar Italian diaspora upon his development creating a daring coming of age narrative about trauma. Bruno writes about the shame and guilt that he endured in his primary relationships resulting in lifelong struggles with self-esteem and identity. His story becomes a compelling example of what John Bowlby has theorized in his famous studies on 'maternal deprivation' and how it thwarts emotional growth (Bretherton, 1992). Over the years, much research has been done in attachment theory which has confirmed that disruptions in a secure connection between mother and child are likely to cause anxiety which can have negative impacts on adult mental health, personality development, future relationships, and ways of coping (Maunder and Hunter, 2015).

Modern psychology unequivocally demonstrates the detrimental effects of poverty and physical, emotional, and sexual abuse on the trajectory of life. These cumulative 'adverse childhood experiences' (ACEs), as originally described by V. J. Felitti (1998), add layers of unhappiness and dysfunction to the adult lives of those who suffered the consequences. An unfortunate result of these adversities is often passed on through generations unless significant insight and healing takes place. More recently, the 2021 book, *Damaged: Childhood Trauma, Adult Illness, and the Need for a Health Care Revolution*, by Robert Maunder and Jonathan Hunter, challenges us to recognize that trauma permeates society. They analyze a patient's relationship with his therapist to demonstrate the pervasive nature of ACEs in a person's life. Fortuitously, Bruno's book is an eloquent illustration of how multiple childhood traumas persist to influence the trajectory of his life, no matter how hard he tries to put them aside.

Bruno had no choice but to learn resilience from an early age. He put it to good use, but paid a high price. He accepted the pain despite his continued efforts to uncover its source. The suppression may well have led to chronic illness. In their 2021 book, *What Happened to You? Conversations on Trauma, Resilience, and Healing*, Bruce Perry and Oprah Winfrey point out that resilience is a coping mechanism that we learn. They write: "We can help each other heal, but often assumptions about resilience and grit blind us to the healing that leads us down the painful path to wisdom" (189). In his memoir, Bruno extends an invitation to us to channel our resilience and join his expedition to unearth remnants of the past. The aim is to help heal the wounds and, hopefully, disrupt the transmission of trauma to future generations.

REFERENCES

Bretherton, I. 1992. "The origins of attachment theory: John Bowlby and Mary Ainsworth." *Developmental Psychology* 28, no. 5 (September): 759–775.

Maunder, Robert and Jonathan Hunter. *Love, Fear, and Health: How our Attachments to Others Shape Health and Health Care.* Toronto: University of Toronto Press, 2015.

Maunder, Robert and Jonathan Hunter. *Damaged: Childhood Trauma, Adult Illness, and the Need for a Health Care Revolution.* Toronto: University of Toronto Press, 2021.

Perry, Bruce D. and Oprah Winfrey. *What Happened to You? Conversations on Trauma, Resilience and Healing.* New York: Flatiron Books, 2021.

ACKNOWLEDGMENTS

WHAT COMES TO MIND, AS I SIT DOWN TO WRITE THIS, IS THE African proverb, "It takes a village to raise a child." The child, in my case, is my memoir, *Mea Culpa: A Plea of Innocence*. And the village is the many individuals that have encouraged me along the way. Without their help, I would not have been able to bring a long gestation to an end. Now that the labor is complete, it feels like I have given birth to a part of me that has been locked deep inside my body.

If I was asked to pick a time where this introspective journey began, it would be late fall, 2004. It was a very low point in my life. I felt desperately alone. My third wife had left me. My parents lived thousands of miles away. Not that I felt a great desire to run to them. My teenage son and I were not on good terms. And, if that wasn't enough, I was struggling financially. The future was bleak. My options limited. Or so I thought.

Somewhere, somehow, I found myself flipping through the pages of an issue of the *Shambhala Sun* magazine when I noticed an advertisement for a Buddhist retreat in a mountain village in south Colorado. The dates—December 4 to January 3—grabbed my attention. I would be away for my birthday, December 11, as well as the Christmas-New Year period. Tailor made! Just for me!

Before the Dathün, the group meditation retreat, I had

never sat on a cushion to meditate. And I knew nothing about Buddhist philosophy and religion. But I signed up anyway, and not for just one or two weeks, but for the whole month!

In meditation and in dreams, I witnessed the release of long-repressed emotions. Anger. Anxiety. Fear. And horror. It was during this catharsis that I saw myself as a defective human being. I discovered a hole in my heart. A hole that I ignored and kept hidden my entire life. Unsuccessfully. I began to familiarize myself with the menacing crater. And, as I did so, I became less afraid and more courageous. I accepted the defect for what it was. Rather than look into darkness in fear, I reversed my gaze and looked into light in hope. And, as I did so, I recognized my mother, in all her sorrow. I walked towards her with out-stretched arms.

I thank *Dr. Reginald "Reggie" Ray* for leading the Dathün that helped me access a well of compassion. This has enabled me to share my bounty with the suffering world around me. And I also thank the members of the Sangha for supporting me during that pivotal period.

Another group that has played a significant role in my awakening, is the Toronto-based men's group, MOSI, or Men Of Serious Intent. To each brave man—*Averill, Bill, Bob, Don, Donato, Doug, Harold, Jack, Mark, Paul, Peeter, Peter, Stephen, Stuart, Tim…*—I offer a humble thank you. Your examples of trust and fearlessness have been a great source of inspiration.

I was trained as an engineer, not as a writer. For helping me hone the latter skill, I thank the many instructors of the creative writing courses at Ryerson University, University of Toronto, University of Victoria, and Camosun College: *Kelli Deeth, Susan Glickman, Allyson Latta, Mary Paterson, Marina Nemat, Beth Kaplan, Faye Ferguson, and Yvonne Blomer.* Your patience and guidance have been exemplary, thank you. And, I also thank the many students I crossed paths with; the feedback you gave me on my writing was and will always be appreciated.

A manuscript is not a book until it is published. To that end, I thank my two "friendly readers," *Patricia Moffat* and *Kris Devon* for their unbiased feedback and encouragement to press on. And, as I continued on the path, I also thank the very talented team of professionals at FriesenPress—*Gillian, Kerry, Alyssa, Kiana*—who helped me cement my vision between two covers!

However, not one word of *Mea Culpa: A Plea of Innocence* would have existed was it not for the endless support and patience from *Dr. Sandra Moffat*, my wife... my editor... my best friend... my lover... my mentor... my confidante... my partner... my everything! Thank you for believing in me.

MORE ABOUT THE AUTHOR

Bruno Cocorocchio was born in 1951 in a small Italian town south-east of Rome. In search of a better life for their children, his parents immigrated to Canada in 1964. In 1974, Bruno graduated with a Bachelor of Applied Science in Electrical Engineering from the University of Toronto.

From graduation to retirement, a span of roughly fifty years, Bruno devoted much effort to the technical discipline for which he had trained while simultaneously developing writing skills. He took courses in scriptwriting and filmmaking, as well as, creative, non-fiction, and memoir writing at Ryerson University, the University of Toronto, and the University of Victoria.

If Bruno's professional life was linear, his personal life was the opposite. He has been married four times:

  – His first marriage was the result of a four-year courtship.

It lasted four months. Youth and naïveté? A story to tell, perhaps.

- The second marriage looked promising, at first. It produced a son and a daughter. Its demise came when his wife died in a car crash. Not an easy story to recount.
- After ten years, his third wife left him when he was at his weakest and too exhausted to pursue her. A story worth telling?
- Finally, Bruno's fourth marriage has, thus far, surpassed all other longevity records. Indication is that it will last till death do them part. Stay tuned.

Currently, Bruno and his wife, Sandra Moffat, live happily in Sidney by the sea on Vancouver Island, British Columbia, Canada.

Honesty was your ideal
Work was your life
Family was your devotion
Your dear ones hold the memory in their hearts
Rest in peace
Amen

Printed in Canada